the BILLION SOUL story

DISCOVERING YOUR ROLE IN GOD'S GOAL

JAMES O. DAVIS

the BILLION SOUL story

DISCOVERING YOUR ROLE IN GOD'S GOAL

Foreword by James Merritt
Afterword by Glenn Burris

The Billion Soul Story:
Discovering Your Role In God's Goal

ISBN: 978-0-9908371-2-1

Billion Soul Publishing
Orlando, Florida
www.billionsoulpub.com

Dedication

The Billion Soul Story
is dedicated to the more than two hundred
Global CoChairs of the Billion Soul Network.
We have learned together that there are riches in niches
and that each of us have a personal role
in God's eternal goal!

Acknowledgments

I would like to take this God-given opportunity to acknowledge the Christ followers who have had a deep impact in the process and production of *The Billion Soul Story: Finding Your Role In God's Goal.*

I will always be grateful for the late Dr. Bill Bright who taught me: "Small dreams will never inflame the hearts of big people. It is always a complement to invite people to accomplish big things for Christ." I could never tell you exactly how many times I hear him teach this visionary principle to me.

Mr. Ralph Lacquement caught the vision and need for *The Billion Soul Story* to be published and invested generously to help bring this timely book to the global Church. We could not have accomplished this without him!

A special thanks to Sheri R. Davis, Emily Conforti, Susan Rhoads, and Kathy Curtis, who provided their editing and layout expertise to help make every word in the manuscript to have deep impact in the reader.

For many years, John Jacobson, managing partner of Riley Warnock & Jacobson in Nashville, Tennessee, has served as legal counsel of the Billion Soul Network. I am deeply grateful for his keen insights, strategic expertise, and incredible friendship!

I am most thankful for Michele Buckingham, who serves as my executive assistant for Cutting Edge International and the Billion Soul Network. She continues to bring world-class execution throughout the Body of Christ.

Words could never express my deepest appreciation for the Cutting Edge International Board of Directors (John Baschieri, vice president; George Sawyer, treasurer; Sheri R. Davis, secretary; Evan Paul, J. Don George, Charles Tuttle, Delbert Smith, and Michael Knight). These visionary leaders have provided collective wisdom and faithful execution throughout the decades.

I would like to express my thanksgiving for George O. Wood, the General Superintendent of the Assemblies of God, in Springfield, Missouri, for his friendship and partnership over the years. He has provided steadfast support through the ups and downs of the Billion Soul Movement.

Evangelism, discipleship, and networking are foundational pillars of Cutting Edge International and the Billion Soul Network. With this in mind, I express my deepest gratitude for the partnerships of John Sorensen, president of Evangelism Explosion; Paul Cole and Joann Webster, president and vice president respectively of the Christian Men's Network; Scott Evans, founder and president of Outreach, Inc.; Elmer Towns, cofounder of Liberty University; Robb Hawks, founder of The Oral Learners Initiative; Mark Sartin, founder of Grace Fellowship Church; and Ben Lerner, founder of Maximized Living.

I stand in awe of the global Christlike diversity throughout the entire Body of Christ today. At the time of this writing, more than two thousand different denominations and organizations have joined synergistic forces to help make it harder for a person to live on this planet and not to hear the glorious Gospel of Jesus Christ. Thank you for your harmonizing servitude throughout the Billon Soul Network!

Contents

FOREWORD

I remember like it was yesterday when the vision of the Billion Soul Network was being cast to the Body of Christ for the very first time. In January 2002, more than five thousand pastors and leaders had chosen to converge at First Baptist Church in Orlando, Florida. This global gathering of the Church took place just four months after the infamous 9/11 in New York City. When a lot of leaders were doubting whether there would be a great attendance, First Baptist was packed with pastors and leaders from all fifty states, every Canadian province, and thirty nations! I was fortunate to bring a keynote message at this conference entitled, *Beyond All Limits.*

Since that initial launch of the Billion Soul Network, I have been fortunate to bring a keynote message at every biennial conference that BSN has hosted in North America. With this mind, I have been able to witness "where we were" then until "where we are" now. I have witnessed firsthand the passion and determination of a visionary who wants to see the Great Commission carried out in his generation.

I have heard Dr. James O. Davis, cofounder of the Billion Soul Network say, "Relational currency is the most valuable currency in the world." Throughout global economies, currencies rise and fall and set the financial standard for the rest of the world. Every day people trade on these currencies for personal and business gain. Yet, I contend that the most valuable traded currencies in the world are not the global currencies (euro, British pound, US dollar, Australian dollar, Chinese renminbi, etc.), but the traded relational currencies between friends and fellow servants, both in the sacred and secular worlds.

Often, during our busy, fast-paced lives we never take the time to evaluate the currency of relationships the Lord has put into our personal lives. If we're not careful we will mistreat or underestimate the value of another person's relationship and not realize how fortunate we are to know them. I contend that we either squander these priceless relationships or invest into them for compounding eternal, Kingdom dividends.

We should invest our time, energy, and resources into cultivating and elevating valuable relationships. Seek out new people along life's journey. From time to time, think through the eyes of your friends and ask yourself, "What can I do to add value to his or her life?" Don't see relationships as stepping-stones but see them as an opportunity to grow mutually together to fulfill the divine destiny in each other's lives for the glory of God. May our prayer be that we recognize the priceless value of these relationships and trade on them with the dignity and respect that bring honor to them and glory to our Lord.

I have often said both publicly and privately that Dr. Davis knows more key Christian leaders than anyone else I know in the global Church today. *The Billion Soul Story* is made up of strategic men and women, from every world region, that have relational ties in this enormous, Kingdom-minded functioning network. At the time of this writing, BSN is comprised of more than two thousand different organizations and more than 500,000 churches in every nation.

As you read *The Billion Soul Story*, you will be encouraged in your heart and enlarged in your mind. You will see the world from a different vantage point by the time you conclude this exciting story. In addition to speaking at the biennial North American conferences, I have been fortunate to network and minister at Billion Soul Summits in different world regions. In *The Billion Soul Story,* you will read about some of the greatest church planters and modern-day history makers in the global Church. Dr. Davis has chosen to wait fifteen years before releasing this powerful, paradigm-shifting, missional read for the Body of Christ. He wanted to complete what he calls "the circumference of Christianity" first so you could experience firsthand a dynamic, heartfelt impact of this global story that is helping to reshape the thinking of millions of pastors and leaders for the fulfillment of the Great Commission in our lifetime.

I can assure you that the greatest currency in the world is the trading of valuable relationships that God places into our lives. I am grateful that Dr. Davis and I met fifteen years ago through the mutual relationship of the late Dr. Bill Bright, founder of Campus Crusade for Christ, when he spoke at the 2001 Southern Baptist Convention. Since that time, we have synergized our relational capital together to make it harder for someone to live on this planet and not hear the glorious Gospel of Christ. I trust as you read *The Billion Soul Story* that you will commit to finding your role in God's goal for this generation.

Dr. James Merritt
President Emeritus
Southern Baptist Convention
Founding Pastor
Cross Pointe Church, Georgia, USA
September 2015

Inspiration: You Can Know It!

The Holy Spirit has placed a billion souls in people's hearts worldwide. On a snowy February 18, 2001, at 2:30 in the afternoon, the Holy Spirit whispered to me to call a renowned Christian leader. I immediately called while driving my car home in Springfield, Missouri. "This is James Davis," I told Charlton, his assistant, "And this call is 8.7 out of a 10 on the Richter scale." Within an hour this distinguished leader called and asked, "James, what is in your heart?" I told him my burden for pastors worldwide. Through my evangelistic travels and ministry, I had learned that more than ninety percent of all ministers worldwide have no formal education. Tens of thousands drop out of ministry each year, and nearly every week I was with another great pastor, listening to the challenges he faced.

One month with many days of fasting passed. In March of 2001 in San Bernardino, California, we met, and a vision was born. In August, he and I announced publicly for the first time before the Assemblies of God Presbytery that we were in partnership to help plant five million new churches for a Billion Soul harvest. That year we worked hard, building a network inspiring others to have eyes to the ends of the earth. We hosted a Beyond All Limits Pastors' Conference in January 2002, with more than five thousand pastors attending from around the world. This conference convened just four months after the infamous World Trade Center disaster took place on September 11, 2001. We were told that no one would come. We were told that we should quit and turn around and go back. We were told that if we were to have this conference, in the context of what was going on in the world, we were sure to fail. I have met more people than I can remember, who have told me that they attended the Beyond All Limits Pastors Conference, and have said that it is one of the best pastors conferences of their life. Don't let the doubters rob you of the dream that God has put in your heart!

On July 11, 2003, my wife Sheri, daughter Olivia, and I saw this mighty man of God for the last time in his Orlando condo. His body was weak but his eyes were bright, and through gasps he admonished me to be faithful to the Lord and the vision. After we'd prayed together, I looked into his eyes for the last time and told this visionary leader that when I saw him next in heaven I would testify that I was faithful to the vision and more than one billion people were saved during our generation.

After more than thirteen years, I have concluded, there is not a price too high, a pain too deep, or problems too big to stop the Billion Soul movement. The popular saying is, "Higher levels, bigger devils," but we press forward to win the second billion to Christ.

Since its inception, the Billion Soul movement has centered around pastors and local churches. When we started, we often said the most important person in every community on earth is not the governor, not the congressman, the senator, or even the president. The most important person in every community is the local Spirit-filled pastor. As goes the pastor, so goes the community.

The Billion Soul movement is not about steeples, but peoples; not about fame, but faith; not about money, but the Master; not about spending, but investing; not about net worth, but network; not about philosophers, but practitioners; not about only the reached, but the unreached; not about ivory towers, but grassroots. We're not about doing old business as usual that did not finish the job. We're about embracing the new face of Christianity, the rise of global Christianity that works together to complete the Great Commission.

In the previous generation, the Western church returned in a great harvest. Today, old maps will not work in new lands. Small doors, however, can open into big rooms. The Billion Soul movement is not about the Western church telling pastors worldwide how to win a billion. We're not about telling others what to do, but asking how we can add value to do it better. We're not about the West headed to the rest, but about the best going to the rest. We're not about the West going to the rest, but the best around the world going to the rest.

The Billion Soul movement believes that every church, regardless of its size, and every Christian, whether known or unknown, can add value to the entire global church.

The Billion Soul movement believes that every church, regardless of its size, and every Christian, whether known or unknown, can add value to the entire global church. The Billion Soul movement is not exclusive, but inclusive. Cynics say the Billion Soul vision is far too big. No, the vision is not too big, but too small. Jesus Christ did not die for a percentage of the world, but He died for the whole world. He did not die just for the second billion, but for the 7.5 billion people on this earth. Let's win them all.

A billion is too big to ignore and too big to do alone. If we're to finish the Great Commission, we cannot care who gets the credit as long as God gets the glory. We must move from *me* to *we* if they will ever hear about *Him*. The Billion Soul Network is not about egos and logos, but about souls,

souls, souls, and more souls. We have to realize collectively that the Great Commission will never be completed simply by proclaiming the Gospel through crusades, literature, compassion, satellite, radio, or Internet, but also by planting churches. Until churches are planted in every unreached area, the devil has a stronghold that defies Christ. Whenever Christians are silent, the devil roars.

The late Adrian Rogers said, "James, it's not whether you know the devil, but does the devil know you?" The Billion Soul movement is about placing the global vision in the hot halls of hell, and announcing to every demonic force, "A billion souls will be saved in our generation." It is about emptying hell and filling up heaven.

The Billion Soul Network is not about adding, but multiplying; not about taking longer, but about finishing the Great Commission even sooner. Should we answer our global challenge in the next ten to fifteen years, we will double the five million churches and one billion Christians in the world today by working together. The overarching goal of the Billion Soul movement is to shorten the time needed to finish the Great Commission by centuries. By 2042, there will be more than nine billion people on this planet. The Billion Soul movement is about doubling the size of the global church and getting ahead of this explosive population curve.

If we do not collectively act now, it will take several more centuries to fulfill the Great Commission. Together, we can make it more difficult each day for a person to go to hell. We can help save billions from being eternally lost. Our generation may not see the Great Commission completed, but the church will be positioned to fulfill the Great Commission by AD 2100. For the first time in history, it is possible for today's preschool children, our children and grandchildren, to live long enough to witness the Gospel being preached to every person.

The Billion Soul movement needs everybody. We don't need elbows jostling for position. We need hands, hearts, and heads serving for the greater good. In 2001, I coauthored *The Synergistic Church* with the late Dr. Bill Bright.

Synergy is at the core of the Billion Soul Network. We can do more with less by multiplying our efforts through working together. It's not just about leadership, but relationship. Completing the Great Commission is not about money. It's about motivation. We have enough money, enough Christians, enough time, enough talent, and enough resources in the Kingdom of God. The reason we have not finished the Great Commission is that we are not motivated. Some would rather turn inward to fight one another than to turn outward to fight alongside each other. The problem is not a *how to,* but a *want to.*

A century ago a missionary missed a ship. It was a missed opportunity by years. Through perilous travel into unknown regions, poor communication, and meager resources, missionaries forged ahead with a rallying cry, "Bring back the King." Where is the passion with which they cried bitter tears for those dying without Christ? Where is the heart tug that pulled them to brave any voyage, go to any jungle, and fight harder with each mounting difficulty? The words of the past generations, on whose shoulders we stand, still echo in the heavenlies, "Bring back the King." The world itself is calling, "Give us truth." We cannot bring back those who bring back the King. We alone are the stewards of those whom we call our own generation.

A small group of executives work together each year to make Mickey Mouse the most recognized name on earth. We have a billion plus Christians on earth. If we want to, we can finish spreading the name above all names, Jesus Christ. More than two billion people do not know the meaning of Christmas or why we celebrate Easter. More than two billion people on the planet do not have a church within walking distance or even one verse of Scripture to read. It must be all hands on deck to save the lost. A church that's not winning the lost is lost itself.

We're asking Christians to put on the whole armor of God—not to watch it shine in the polished mirrors of fellowship halls, but to watch it work in the battle to win the second billion.

God birthed the Billion Soul Network. We're moving forward to build it worldwide. Even though this network began with just two leaders from two totally different streams of Christianity, at the time of this writing, there are more than two thousand Christian organizations synergizing their efforts together, along with 500,000 churches worldwide. The Lord is challenging us to become part of something bigger than ourselves. We're asking Christians to put on the whole armor of God—not to watch it shine in the polished mirrors of fellowship halls, but to watch it work in the battle to win the second billion. One day, the King of the universe will ascend through eternity into time, walking on clouds, the diadem of glory on His head and a rainbow of victory wrapped around His shoulders, and from the celestial shores of heaven we will look back across our lives and realize that the Lord did not promise us smooth sailing, but a safe landing.

In heaven, we can no longer win souls. We will be unable to accomplish the very goal for which Jesus died. All of heaven is cheering us to win a billion souls. We need to be motivated about what motivates heaven. How many souls will you be responsible for? How many churches will you help to plant? One can put a thousand to fight, but two can put ten thousand to fight. We can achieve more together than we could alone by synergizing our efforts to bring back the King.

1

Embracing What God Has Raised Up

Where there is no vision; the people are unrestrained,
But happy is he who keeps the law.
—Proverbs 29:18

I remember on one occasion in the summer of 2002, we had a breakfast meeting for potential donors to come and hear the vision of online training and synergistic partnerships for the future. One particular short-sighted leader spoke up and said, "James, what about the Island nations in the South Pacific? These nations have no Internet. This global vision you are articulating will not work there."

I never forgot that moment, listening to this person intentionally casting doubt in the minds of the leaders who were in the meeting. My intelligent response to this ludicrous comment was, "When NASA was launching the first rocket to the moon, they did not ask where the moon was, but where the moon would be when the rocket arrived there. It does not matter how great your rocket is if you are not able to project into the future."

This is the same answer I give to the critics today who say that the Great Commission will not be completed in our lifetime. When I look across the landscape of time and see who our Lord is raising up, I have no doubt the Great Commission will be finished in our lifetime or at least during this generation.

Look at what has happened before our eyes. Four percent of Christianity is in North America, and 96 percent is scattered all over the world. For those living in the West, this statistic tells us that we know very little about the global church today. If you live in the United States and pay attention to what God is doing only in your region, you'll be aware of a mere 4 percent of what is happening in Christianity throughout the globe. If you're a member of a global denomination or fellowship of churches, you can gain an understanding of that group's maximum missional reach throughout the rest of the world, and then at best you may be familiar with an approximately eight percent of what Christianity is doing throughout the world.

Now let's say that you study Christianity fully in North America, including your own tribe, and then you expand your research to include still another denomination or fellowship. This might lead you to a pretty comprehensive understanding of the ministry and mission of Christians that make up ten to twelve percent of the entire global church. However, there is still a whopping ninety percent of followers and churches of Jesus Christ in the world today that remain unfamiliar to you and your church or denomination.

When we step back into church history to the year 1900, we find that 45.69 percent of the world at that time was evangelized for Christ. Even after great missionary initiatives where the goal was to complete the Great Commission by the turn of that century, a full 55 percent of the world still had never heard the Gospel for the first time. By the year 2000, 73.09 percent of the world had been evangelized. On the surface that looks like the Church had made great progress toward fulfilling the Great Commission because such a much higher percentage of people heard the Gospel at least one time. At a current rate of evangelism, by the year 2200, 83.25 percent of the world will have been evangelized. It sounds like real progress, but there is a huge catch.

The problem is that world population is growing exponentially. In 2011 the world population passed seven billion people, of which 2.4 billion went unreached. By 2050 it is estimated that there will be 9.5 billion people on the planet, of which two billion people will be unreached. So, even though the church is growing faster than ever before and in many places in the world surpassing the birthrate, we come to an understanding as to where the church is worldwide, where the church is going, and find out synergistic ways to serve one another. This century will come and go without growing any closer to fulfilling the mandate of the Great Commission.

By 2100 there could be at least eleven billion people alive, and 1.8 billion will be unreached. This means that in roughly a hundred years at the present rate, the number of people needing to hear the Gospel for the very first time will have decreased by 600 million people. However, the problem that should concern all of us is that, after a hundred years of the most rapid rise of global communications in world history, one hundred years of investment and sacrifice, one hundred years of funding and sending, we will still be nowhere closer to fulfilling the Great Commission Jesus gave us more than two thousand years ago.

One day in 2005, God spoke to my heart as I was playing with my oldest daughter. It was a lighthearted moment, so I was surprised that I felt Him press me with these words, "Go and see the mountains that I have raised up around the world." That's when I began to research what the Lord was doing from the many different streams of Christianity. I had a strong interest for more than ten years to know more and more about the body of Christ, but it was in that defining moment I decided I would try to find out what the Lord had raised up all over the world.

When I followed through on what the Lord had challenged me to do, I was able to see the mountaintops all over the world that God had raised up. We met with giants of the faith, people who had planted hundreds of churches, pastors of gigantic churches, leaders of denominations we had never heard of, leaders whose Western counterparts were far smaller than those overseas. We just didn't know before we went what we would find.

I have never been more excited about the potential of the Church of Jesus Christ to fulfill the Great Commission than I am today.

Several years ago my wife Sheri and I went to Europe and had the opportunity to look around between ministry assignments. One day I found myself standing in the middle of a beautiful sanctuary in an area where there had been several wars. It was a gorgeous reminder of the cathedral's former glory when thousands had come there to worship. As I stood looking at what once was, I realized that our faith in God and His character determine how we respond to Him. If our faith and knowledge in the Scripture tell us that the Lord is with us and that He is good and merciful, then we will move closer to Him when difficulty or hardship comes into our lives. However, if we've come to the conclusion that Christ is not present, that He's far off and not able to save us when difficulties arrive, we will blame Him and move further away from His saving grace.

I have never been more excited about the potential of the Church of Jesus Christ to fulfill the Great Commission than I am today. The possibility of God's mission being accomplished in this generation is real. In the world today there are more than 30,000 denominations and fellowships, more than 1.4 billion Protestants, more than 1.1 billion Catholics, more than 100,000 new Christian converts per day, and more than 1,000 Christians planted each day throughout the world, especially in the East and South. We are living in an age where past paradigms are giving way to global visions and life stories. As a result, it is no longer the West that is going to the rest, but in increasing numbers, there are people from many other regions going to the lost throughout the world.

For more than two hundred years the Western church has done a phenomenal job funding and training the church world. The United States in particular has played a major part in the furtherance of the Gospel. In our generation we've helped spread Christianity to the four corners of the earth. The smallest child collecting pennies from missionaries has helped. Our large churches with massive mission budgets have helped. Young couples sacrificially heading off into the mission field, taking children who will never really know their grandparents, have helped.

The result is that the global church has grown up. The global church is not an immature church; the global church is a maturing church. We are witnessing the rise of global Christianity, and though there is still an enormous amount of work to be done, particularly among unreached people groups, the global church is advancing faster today than ever before.

We in the West must now move from parenting to partnering. Think about how we live our Christian lives. It is not dissimilar to how we live our natural lives. The majority of people in the world will never travel outside their country of origin. A large percentage will never live more than a few hundred miles from their birthplace. Most of us in the global church have grown up around our own silo. We walk in the footsteps of those who've come before us, and we stand on the shoulders of past generations in order to build on their foundation. This paradigm has allowed us to grow but has limited our vision to the walls of our own silos. The Holy Spirit of Christ is focused on illuminating the world—not spotlighting our silos.

If we just want to grow a church or to multiply a group of churches, or even strengthen our spiritual tribe or denomination, then silo living is fine and we can achieve that goal right where we are. But to live the Great Commission we're going to have to get out of our own silos, find out what God is doing in the rest of the harvest field, and set our hands to the plow in new and extraordinary ways. Old maps will not work in new lands.

In regard to the Great Commission, this is our decade, this is our century, this is our present age— this is the only moment we have.

Christian churches focused on making the shift from silo to silo are going to ride a ministry tide that is unlike anything we've seen in history. Those who choose to continue to go it alone rather than working together with others in the global community may enjoy a somewhat gradual incline. But if they do not take part in the excitement of God's global mission, they will not experience God's awesome and saving power within the Church that can lift and change the world.

What got us here will not take us there. What brought the Gospel of Jesus Christ to where we are today will not be the same methodology that takes the Gospel to all the world tomorrow. The working done in the past must give way to the networking in order to reach people groups for Christ.

Remarkable Christian leaders are now making this shift in their churches to move from production to reproduction. The missional tide of global Christianity began to change and rise in the 1980s and 1990s. This tide has caused a global seismic shift, the greatest in the history of Christianity. The more that Christians everywhere can take ownership of our own Lord's assignment, the more the Holy Spirit can move among us, urging us away from Western vision toward a shared global mission, and moving us away from personal goals into missional roles.

In the future there will be more and more missionaries in the world who rise up from within the countries outside of the West. We Westerners must realign our mission with God's global mission, or we will be left behind.

One afternoon while I was speaking to Rich DeVos, who founded the Amway Corporation during a poor economic period, I asked him why he started the company during such a bad decade of business. He answered, "It was the only decade I had." In regard to the Great Commission, this is our decade, this is our century, this is our present age—this is the only moment we have. I'm often asked, "Do you really believe that the Great Commission can be fulfilled or completed in this century?" My response is always, "This is the only century we have." We have to finish it now. This is the only lifetime any of us have. We can't predict what only God can do, but we can step in with what He is doing. When we do we'll go further than we've ever dreamed possible.

2

Getting Ahead of the Population Curve

When Jesus approached Jerusalem,
He saw the city and wept over it.
—Luke 19:41

In January 2004, we hosted the Beyond All Limits 2 pastors' conference in Orlando, Florida. I was told by several well-known leaders that we would be fortunate if "two thousand pastors" attend this particular conference. One specific leader and author said, "The only reason why five thousand pastors came to Beyond All Limits 1 in 2002 was because Bill Bright, founder of Campus Crusade For Christ, had invited them." With this in mind, I simply pulled our team together, marketed worldwide, and 6,200 pastors and leaders joined us! And by the way, when we crossed two thousand in attendance, I casually sent an e-mail to this leader mentioned above, letting him know that his prophecy did not come to pass. It was at the Beyond All Limits 2 conference where we brought concrete clarity to the vision of "five million new churches for a billion soul harvest."

We worked hard throughout the year of 2004. In December 2004, approximately fifty global leaders met via conference call to synergistically discuss and decide the next steps needed worldwide to pull together the entire body of Christ for five million new churches and for a billion soul harvest. As we collectively moved into 2005, Kingdom-minded invitations were issued to key leaders serving the Lord in every major denomination, to join us for the first-ever Global Church Planting Congress in Dallas, Texas. Against all natural odds, in September 2005, five hundred significant leaders synergized their efforts together at the Global Church Planting Conference and the "Billion Soul Initiative" was launched throughout the Global Church.

It took us four years, from the first time we cast the vision of five million churches for a billion souls, before we had gained enough knowledge to be able to develop an international strategy of success. At the time of this writing, more than three million churches have been planted and 700 million people have come to Christ. These statistics are the result of the compounding global averages provided through the more than 240 CoChairs of the Billion Soul Network. We are on course to cross five million new churches for a billion soul harvest in the year of 2020.

Why a second billion now? Sixty thousand babies were born in India last night. You may say, "What does that have to do with me?" It has nothing to do with you if you're not interested in telling this whole world about Jesus. It has nothing to do with you if you're not completely interested in finishing your God-given assignment. It has nothing to do with you if you do not have a circumference vision that incorporates the entire world. Sixty thousand babies may not sound like much at first, but in just twenty short days, you have a million people.

Population is expanding exponentially every day. This is what makes the Great Commission extremely difficult. I realize there are political issues. I realize there are social issues. I realize there are cross-cultural issues. But the dark and stark reality is that for centuries the Church has chased population but it has never gotten ahead of that population.

Oftentimes we as fellow leaders cast vision in terms like this: *Let's reach this generation for Christ*. Over the last ten years

I have come to the conclusion that it's time for us to cast vision in terms of: *Let's prepare to reach the generation that is not yet here.* In other words, let's think about where population is growing, think about where population is going, and let's cast vision, for the first time, to get ahead of it.

Let's prepare to reach the generation that is not yet here.

Oftentimes businesses make proposals which predict where growth and growth cycles will be. They make plans ahead of time, even before there is a product or a customer interested in the product. So I suggest that we cast vision ahead of the population curve. In less than ten years from the time of this writing there will be more than eight billion people on the planet. The Church has found it difficult to finish the Great Commission when there was six billion, when there was five billion, and now seven billion have come and gone.

Oftentimes the Church is the slowest institution on the planet. I suggest that we ought to be the sharpest, the most efficient, the most creative, the most equipped visionary leaders of any organization in the world to finish the assignment which we have been placed on this planet to fulfill. In this same generation, we're going to witness nine billion and more. With this in mind, I suggest that we synergistically think about how we can reach the eight billion or the nine billion and make plans accordingly now, instead of constantly chasing the population growth.

The Billion Soul Movement is about doubling the size of the global church and getting ahead of population growth so that we can finish the Great Commission in the twenty-first century. We believe there is a window of time in which together we can synergistically get ahead of the population and hopefully finish the Great Commission by the year AD 2100. If it's not going to be now, then when is it going to be?

It seems like in the last ten to fifteen years the Holy Spirit has whispered a memo throughout the body of Christ. Basically, what the Holy Spirit has said is, "Stop fighting one another and focus on what I've asked you to do." I grew up in a Pentecostal tradition, but I can tell you some of my closest friends in all the world are not part of my Pentecostal family. I thank God for the diversity in the body of Christ. It is not that we need to surrender our distinctives in order to finish our assignment; it is that we can celebrate who the Lord has made us to become in Him . Then we can go out and finish what He has called us to do.

Dr. Glenn Burris, president of Foursquare International, articulates it this way, "We all have a common enemy. It is the devil. It is not our brother or our sister. We all have a common Savior. His name is Jesus. And we all have a common assignment. That's fulfilling the Great Commission." It is not that we choose to prefer one stream of Christianity more than another stream of Christianity. It is, rather that we need to find common ground working together so we might achieve what all of us have been commissioned and challenged to do.

In July of 2003, my wife, our oldest daughter, Olivia, and I were in Iowa for a Chinese reunion. We had not yet adopted our second child, Priscilla. From time to time we have met with certain individuals to celebrate the adoption of our Chinese daughters. While we were in Des Moines, an event took place that I will never forget. We were in the hotel room preparing to go out to dinner when my cell phone began to ring. When I looked down, I saw that it was the late Dr. Adrian Rogers giving me a call. I thought to myself, *Oh no. Did I do anything wrong?*

Dr. Rogers was actually calling just to express his love and appreciation for me. He articulated over the phone that he'd been praying for me, and he'd been giving God praise for

my life. Of course, I didn't feel worthy, and I still don't feel worthy when anyone speaks such things, but Dr. Rogers went on to say, "James, you grew up in the Assemblies of God. I grew up in the Southern Baptist Convention. You grew up in a Pentecostal tradition, but I did not." Then, he said, "I just want to say thank you for never making me feel like a second-class citizen. I have watched you as you have served my beloved friend, Dr. Bill Bright. I have watched you as you have helped him do whatever he needed done in the twilight years of his life. You have washed his hands like Elisha washed Elijah's hands, and I have concluded that you are a dear brother in Christ." This is one of the greatest compliments I've ever received in my life.

Instead of getting closer to the one, which only has a value of ten, go to the end of the line and have a value of a billion.

But the reason I highlight that story is not even for one second to articulate self-aggrandizement, but to illustrate the point that we can, as brothers and sisters in Christ, serve with one another in great value to achieve something greater than ourselves. Yet in order for this to be achieved, there must be a servant mentality, one who defers to his or her brother instead of always jostling to be at the front of the line. In the Billion Soul Movement we teach that the last zero has the most value. Instead of getting closer to the one, which only has a value of ten, go to the end of the line and have a value of a billion.

We can reach the second billion in this generation. Why do we need to do it now? We need to do it because of the population explosions all over the world. We need to do it because the Holy Spirit is quickening people's hearts to synergize together, mobilize together, analyze together, and strategize together in order to evangelize together and disciple this generation for Christ. But I also think of the technological advancements. It is simply beyond comprehension what is taking place in our world today.

In June 2001, I was in Bangkok, Thailand, with a missionary friend, Dr. Ronald Maddux. Dr. Maddux and I have been friends since the 1980s. Along with me on this missions trip were Pastor John Baschieri and Pastor George Sawyer. John and George are founding pastors of New Life Assembly, Lehigh, Florida; and Calvary Assembly, Decatur, Alabama, respectively. While in Bangkok, we received a call from Missionary Maddux to travel by bus from the hotel to his office. Throughout the decades I have been careful as to how to I travel when in a country outside of the United States. At any rate, a divine revelation was about to happen on this Bangkok city bus!

When George, John, and I boarded the bus, we had to sit on the last row due to the overcrowded conditions. Bangkok is always hot due to its location near the equator, and it was scorching in the back of the bus. Just prior to leaving on this trip, Dr. Bill Bright, founder of Campus Crusade in Orlando, met with me regarding the future of online training worldwide. During our meeting, he gave me a short five-minute video clip, "Red Sky in the Morning," that could be uploaded to a PalmPilot. Today, PalmPilots don't exist, and it is possible that you may not even know what I am talking about. As the digital revolution was picking up speed in the late 1990s, many people carried a cell phone and also a planning device (PalmPilot, etc.) One was for calls and the other was for scheduling and lists. Today, these two devices have become one, the smart phone.

While I was sitting in the back of this Bangkok bus with loud noise all around me, I uploaded "Red Sky in the Morning" to my PalmPilot. I could hear and see the video, even though it was choppy and not completely clear on my handheld device. Then, a divine revelation came to me. The

Holy Spirit twice whispered to me these words, "They will study like this one day." While I was watching the video, I received a vision of the future of online, handheld training.

The technological advancements have made it possible for us to win the second billion faster and more effectively than ever before.

I remember when we announced the vision in 2002 before five thousand people at First Baptist Church in Orlando, Florida. We articulated that one day more people would study across the Internet than in all the colleges and universities throughout the world. I'm sure on that occasion there were some people who snickered under their breath and said, "Dreamer, dream on." Yet today that is reality. At the time of this writing, nearly fifty thousand pastors/leaders are taking training courses in the Global Church Learning Center (www.GCLC.tv).

We are experiencing the greatest technological advancements of all time. Think about this for a moment. In 1969 when the astronauts landed on the moon, all they had was a forty-megabyte computer in their spaceship. Today, forty megabytes will get you nowhere. Our handheld devices today will hold between fifty and one hundred gigabytes of information.

At the time of this writing, information is doubling every eighteen months. The day will come when information will double every year. Then the day will come that it will double every six months, every month, every week, and, ultimately, every day. Can you imagine getting up one day and saying, "I'm caught up in my understanding," and then the next day you're halfway behind again? The technological advancements have made it possible for us to win the second billion faster and more effectively than ever before. But it's not just the winning. It is making disciples where disciples make disciples; where disciples are equipped to win more.

We need to win the second billion and double the size of the church. Winning the second billion gives every tribe of Christianity the opportunity to add value to one another, while at the same time adding eternal value toward the fulfillment of the Great Commission. One of the greatest satisfactions in life is helping people achieve something that they could not do by themselves.

3

Saving the World One Billion at a Time

The fruit of the righteous is a tree of life,
And he who is wise wins souls.
—Proverbs 11:30

In the fall of 2007, Leonard Sweet and I were sitting in a restaurant in Morristown, New Jersey. In our conversation, he asked me, "What do you hope to do or accomplish in the next decade ahead of you?" I lightly said, "I hope I can help change the world." His response to me was something I can never forget as long as I live. In a few simple words he said to me, "God hasn't called you to change the world. He's called you to save it." I'll never forget it. God called me to save it.

Have you thought about that? God has called you to save this world, not to change this world. You see, the Bible says that Jesus came to seek and to save. It is Jesus who does the saving, and the change comes out of the saving. For too long Christians have articulated and believed that, as we go, change really comes. But in reality, Christ was already doing work before we ever got there. He didn't call us to change it; he called us to save it. If we can change people into something else, then someone else can come along and change them once again. You might say that we're splitting hairs and we're saying more and more about less and less. Yet I contend there is a fundamental difference between saving the world and changing the world.

There have been many entrepreneurs in the world who've brought change. There have been many leaders, both good and bad, who have brought change. But none of them have brought salvation. There is change that comes after salvation, but it's not because we did it; it is because Christ did it in them. It is because Christ did it in us. When a person is drowning in a lake or a river or an ocean, he or she does not say, "Come over here and change me." They say, "Come over here and save me."

God has called you to save this world, not to change this world.

Let me explain it to you this way. Steve Jobs, the founder of Apple, was truly one of the greatest change agents of all time. When Steve Jobs passed away, from all outward appearances at least, he died lost. Steve Jobs had a Hindu philosophy that motivated his life. When he passed away, he died lost. Shortly after his passing, a book about his life came out, but I was never motivated to read it. The reason I couldn't read it is because I realized this gentleman, for all outward appearances, died lost. Please do not think that I even suggest that I can positively know when a person lives or when he dies where his eternal destiny will be. But the Bible does teach us that you will know them by their fruit. Bad root, bad shoot, bad fruit.

Even though Steve Jobs was one of the greatest entrepreneurial change agents in the world, he did not save the world. Some consider Mr. Jobs on the level of Henry Ford, Thomas Edison, and other great inventors and entrepreneurs. When you think of an iPhone, iTunes, iPads, Apple, and the technological advancements, you think of Mr. Steve Jobs. He brought phenomenal change to this world, but he did not save this world. When you think of Osama bin Laden and other mean, devilish-spirited men or women, you will also come to the conclusion that, yes, they brought change to this world, but they did not save this world.

We've not been called to change it; we've been called to save it. Realizing this causes us to have a deeper humility and a greater dependency upon the power of the Holy Spirit flowing in and through our lives.

We will never accomplish what we have been called to accomplish by simply thinking that we "have all the goods," and we can do it by ourselves. We will never succeed in saving this planet. Only Jesus Christ, through us, can achieve that in any generation. Since there are currently more than a billion Christians in this world, the reality is that the next billion lives next door. In other words, if the billion Christians on the planet simply won a neighbor, we would double the size of the global church.

So let's say we gave everybody a ten-year goal to simply win one person. Is this reasonable? Of course it's reasonable. Is it reasonable to believe that every Christian in the world can win one in five years? Of course it is. We could take a run at it in a week. However, for the sake of mathematical computation, the next billion Christians simply live next door. As long as it takes to win our neighbors is the same time it takes to win a billion!

If we would simply reach a neighbor, no matter where we find ourselves—whether it be in the Middle East, South America, North America, Asia, or wherever it may be—we could simply lead him or her to Jesus Christ. Every once in a while I hear someone say, "The reason I don't give my best to Jesus Christ is I'm afraid He might call me to a distant land and I don't want to do that." My response is simply, "If you can't cross the street for your neighbor, do you think He's going to trust you to cross the sea for a nation?"

In recent years, I've been pondering the global footprint of Christianity and it's taken me a while to come to the realization that Christ has been strategically planting His body all over the world. Let me explain it to you this way. I remember in the summer of 1975 when the Holy Spirit was quickening my heart and calling me into full-time ministry. It was during that time I felt the Lord was calling me to be a preacher of the Gospel in my generation. I remember surrendering my will at a Friday night youth service where I said to the Lord, "Lord, I'll go wherever You want me to go. I'll become who You want me to become." And with tears flowing down my cheeks, I surrendered my life into ministry. I knew from that point on I was going to be a preacher of the Gospel and I needed to prepare my life for such a divine assignment. Since that glorious evening, I have never doubted my sacred calling one time!

And yet I come to the this conclusion—that the Lord did the same thing in the hearts of other men and women from different strains of Christianity, whether they be Pentecostal, evangelical, denominational or interdenominational. The same Lord who reached in and saved my heart and called me into full-time ministry also reaches into the hearts of other men and women in different strains of Christianity, saves them, and calls them into full-time ministry. Their divine call is no less than mine and my divine call is no less than theirs.

When God called me and thrust me out, He would also call them and thrust them out. Maybe it was different for them than it was for me, but that call of God was just as sacred for them as it was for me. My role has been different than theirs, and their role has been different than mine. Their location may be one location for their whole life; mine may be one of travel, teaching, preaching, and networking. But it doesn't mean that one calling is greater than another calling.

Over the last two hundred years or so, the Lord has been sending men and women out to the four corners of the earth. They've gone to the easy places and the hard places, to the small places and the big places. They've evangelized, discipled, and planted churches, and the Lord has done societal transformation through their lives. The Lord has sent them, and where they have planted, the church has grown. Therefore, in reality, Christianity is where it is today in the world because the Lord sent His servants to go and to preach and teach there. If that's true—and it is—there has been a divine design behind where the global church is today.

Whether we live in Cambodia, Chile, or Canada, if we are Christ's followers, there are other people in close proximity who need to know the Lord.

Having said that, it means that we respect where the Lord has planted our fellow servants throughout the body of Christ and we choose to learn where they are and who they are rather than pretend that there's no one else that's following Jesus Christ. What got us there in the past will not bring us where we need to be in the future. When I say the next billion lives next door, it really does. Whether we live in Cambodia, Chile, or Canada, if we are Christ's followers, there are other people in close proximity who need to know the Lord. All of us have neighbors who desperately need to come to a saving knowledge of Christ.

I could not begin to tell you how many international trips I have taken over the last fourteen years. In 2005, I flew to Suva, Fiji, for a two-hour meeting with Rev. Suliasi Kurulo. Pastor Kurulo is the founding pastor of the World Harvest Center, the largest and strongest church in Oceania. Over the last twenty-five years, through his leadership, more than 5,100 churches have been planted in 115 nations! I did not travel to Fiji to preach or teach, but simply to get to know one of the greatest Christian leaders of our generation.

In 2008, I jumped on a plane in Orlando, Florida, in order to fly through Atlanta and on to Lagos, Nigeria. My dear friend, Dr. Ademola Ishola, is the president emeritus of the Nigerian Baptist Convention. Upon my arrival into Lagos, a person helped me into a ministry van and then we drove four hours to where Dr. Ishola and his pastors were having a conference. I traveled all the way there from Orlando and back for a fifteen-minute speech to be given to the pastors who had attended the Nigerian Baptist Convention! You may be tempted to say, "That is a waste of time and resources." Yet, in the final analysis it is all about building Kingdom-minded relationships to prepare us together for future harvest.

How big is your neighborhood? By the term, "neighborhood," I am not thinking about the traditional neighborhood, where there are houses lined up and down a street. I am thinking about the people the Lord has placed in your life. With our neighbors, we can witness to people worldwide and see an unprecedented harvest! When was the last time you led a lost soul to Christ and began discipling him/her to follow Christ?

4

Mobilizing the Best to the Rest of Our World

You will receive power when the Holy Spirit has come upon you; and you shall be My witnesses both in Jerusalem, and in all Judea and Samaria, and even to the remotest part of the earth.
–Acts 1:8

In 2006 while I was in Prague contemplating whether we wanted to have a future Billion Soul Summit there, I made plans to visit Lisbon, Portugal. I had always wanted to go to Portugal but never really had the opportunity to do so. I flew over and spent the night in Lisbon with the intention of getting up the next morning and going to Palos, Spain.

We left at 5:00 a.m. in order to arrive in Palos, Spain, by 9:00 a.m. After arriving, the first thing I did was go to a monastery. In this monastery were ancient artifacts from a different generation. While I was there, I wanted to visit a specific room relating to Christopher Columbus. It was a small room, maybe eight feet by ten feet. As I walked into this small room, across the top of the door were these words, "The Birthplace of America."

Well, as an American, I had always been taught the birthplace of America was Plymouth Rock, Massachusetts. As I walked into this small room, I began to take it all in. I saw there were two chairs with a small table between them. Off to the right was an old picture of Christopher Columbus hanging on the wall. I went in and sat in this chair, the same chair where Christopher Columbus would have sat in 1491.

On some previous occasion, Christopher Columbus would have occupied this chair, and in the other chair was a Franciscan monk. This monk would hear the vision of Christopher Columbus talking about finding the New World and new trade routes. Columbus would also have articulated the need to go around the tip of Africa and then sail across the Atlantic Ocean.

Of course, in that time frame it was unthinkable to consider going a different route because philosophers and scientists believed there were big dragons in the waters, and that you could sail right off the edge because the world was flat. Now, even though they had a wrong worldview and an inadequate paradigm, that was the still the belief of the day.

Christopher Columbus shared his vision with that Franciscan monk, and that Franciscan monk went to the queen of Spain, who went to the king of Spain, and they decided to fund the vision of Christopher Columbus. It was in that small room where the vision got from one man into another.

Christopher Columbus was born in Italy and raised in Portugal. He had already gone to the king and queen of Portugal, but they had dismissed the big idea. I've often wondered if the Portuguese leader would have welcomed the opportunity to reconsider and take Christopher Columbus up on his exploratory plans.

Christopher Columbus is considered one of the greatest explorers the world has ever known. He's listed in the top five of all explorers. His idea was one of the greatest ideas anyone had ever had. Now, of course, when Christopher Columbus set sail, he was trying to make it to India. He didn't realize that he didn't make it to India at first, but he made it to North America. That's why oftentimes the Native Americans are called Indians when in fact they are Native Americans. The vision that Christopher Columbus had literally shook the entire world.

Besides visiting this room, I also visited a Catholic church which is more than a thousand years old. This location where the water banks up against an old rocky wall is the exact place where Christopher Columbus would have put his three boats into the water to set sail for the New World.

I remember kneeling at a beautiful fountain in this grassy area on a gorgeous sunny day. I asked the Lord to double the size of the church in my generation and make it harder for people to live on the planet and not hear the glorious Gospel of Jesus Christ. It was a tremendous, moving time in Palos, Spain.

We are living in a time when old paradigms are passing away and where old worldviews are crashing on the seashore of time.

I knocked on the door of the old Catholic church. The caretaker for the church was a lady who didn't speak much English, so my driver, who spoke fluent Spanish, convinced her to let me go inside. I went inside to the old altar rail where Christopher Columbus and his men would have dedicated their voyage to the Lord and then return some months later to give victory and praise to God.

Now I'm not here to advocate that Christopher Columbus was a perfect man by any stretch of the imagination. But what I do want to communicate is that the vision in his heart was not the common vision of the day. Eventually it would become the vision of the day, and one ship after another ship after another ship would follow in the footsteps of Christopher Columbus. However, when he first took that voyage into the unknown, no one really believed that much would come out of it.

We are living in a time when old paradigms are passing away and where old worldviews are crashing on the seashore of time. We're living in what I call the circumference of Christianity. The world is not flat, and Christianity is not flat. I realize that technological advancements have flattened out the world and that we're more interconnected today than we've ever been before. In fact, I do believe it has been the rise of the Internet that has helped the networking mind-set to develop throughout the body of Christ.

Before the emergence of the Internet, we didn't hear phrases like, "Can I connect with you tomorrow?" "Let's get connected," "Can I network with you?" or Let's network together." You heard it a little, but you did not hear it very often. So I do believe the rise of the Internet has helped men and women to be willing to connect and interconnect more in partnerships than ever before. But there is a circumference of Christianity. The Gospel that has gone out has come back.

I think of key leaders in the West who are in their sunset years. They have believed in their generation that they would be the ones who would finish the Great Commission. They were absolutely convinced of it, but their generation has come and it's almost gone. And many of them who are still with us have come to the conclusion that it won't be done in their lifetime. But it could possibly be done in their children's lifetime or their grandchildren's lifetime.

The circumference of Christianity is simply that the mission field has become a mission force. It's no longer the West going to the rest, but the best around the world going to the rest of the world. What we've all taught in the Billion Soul Network is the global church going to the global church. It almost sounds like we may not know what we're talking about, but there is a 360-degree vision.

It is the fact that men and women throughout the body of Christ are going everywhere today. We have Latino leaders from South America by the thousands who are going to Asia to preach and teach the Gospel. We have Chinese and Asians who are leaving their area of the world. They're going to Europe, America, and Africa. Why? To preach and teach and tell the world about Jesus. We're living in the greatest time of human history where the Gospel is intersecting on all four corners of the earth.

In my generation, when I was approximately thirteen years old, we used to wear a bracelet made out of a thin metal, engraved with these letters: W-W-J-D. As I have traveled over time, all I have to mention is W-W, and the audience can finish J-D. And it simply means: "What would Jesus do?" So if you found yourself in a situation and you wondered what you should say or what you should do, the goal was for you to ponder what Jesus would do. The implication also is, *Well, He's not here, but if He was, what would He do?* It was kind of like: He used to walk among us. He used to teach among us. And if He was here, what would He say? What would He do?

I suggest that we need a new bracelet, and it should be W-I-J-D: "What is Jesus doing?" That's what's so exciting about the Billion Soul Network. One of the missions of the Billion Soul Network is to find out what Jesus is doing and connect those people together. We need to find out what the Lord is already doing and then connect these various leaders together.

Many Christians have the idea that Jesus wasn't really doing that much before we got there, and yet that could not be further from the truth. Just the other day I was working on a letter, and I said a sentence that I so often use. It was something like, "Let's go out and do something for Jesus Christ," or "Let's go out and do something significant for Jesus Christ." But now I've begun to rephrase my sentence. Instead of going out and doing something *for* Him, let's go out and do something *with* Him. Let's go out and work and serve with Jesus with what He's already doing in the world through the person of the Holy Spirit. Rather than thinking we're breaking new ground, let's just simply go out *with* Him and believe for supernatural results.

We are truly living in the circumference of Christianity. As Christianity develops some sense of maturity in a culture, the natural tendency is for that same culture to take it for granted. And as soon as we take it for granted even by one percent, we're already slipping in the wrong direction.

Instead of going out and doing something for Him, let's go out and do something with Him.

I want to ask you, what kind of frequency are you listening to? Are you listening to W-I-F-M? W-I-F-M is simply: What's in it for me? Are you getting up every day asking yourself, *What's in it for me?* Do you only go as far as what is in it will take you? Or have you decided that you will change the frequency and move to W-I-F-J: What's in it for Jesus?

Years ago, William Edward Perry, a famous English explorer, mapped out most of the southern polar cap. Many of his maps are still being used today by those who travel to that desolate, subzero continent. On one particular expedition, he and his crew, having mapped an uncharted region, were preparing to hike to another unfamiliar location. On the eve of their departure, they studied the stars and determined their exact coordinates. As the sun rose, they began a hard, lengthy journey north to this unmapped region. They marched through the ice and snow all day long with the freezing air burning their lungs. As the sun set, they made camp, totally exhausted from their trip.

After their evening meal, Mr. Perry studied the stars again to determine their exact coordinates. He was stunned to learn that even though he and his crew had journeyed north all day, they were now further south than when they began in the morning. After struggling to solve this problem, they discovered that even though they had traveled north, they were on a giant ice flow that was moving faster south than they were moving north. While they thought they were going in the right direction, they were slip sliding away and did not even know it.

A deeply sobering reality is that it is possible for a leader's organization to grow numerically and flourish financially; but while thinking at the same time he is making great strides in the right direction, he is actually losing ground each year. There are countless numbers of Christians who have not slowed down long enough to assess whether they are truly helping to fulfill the Great Commission. The Billion Soul story is filled with pastors and people who have chosen to check future coordinates that align themselves toward crossing the finish line, sharing the Gospel with those in "reached" and "unreached" regions.

5

Utilizing the Internet to Equip Your Global Team

But as for you, Daniel, conceal these words and seal up the book until the end of time; many will go back and fourth, and knowledge will increase.
—Daniel 12:4

At the risk of showing my age, do you remember the early dial-up days of the Internet? Do you remember having to plug in one end of a cord into your computer and the other end into a wall outlet? If you do, then you jumped on the Internet during its ramp-up timeframe. I remember like it was yesterday in 1996, becoming a charter member of America Online, with a dial-up speed of ultimately 36K or 56K! Today no matter where you may be in the world you will never find this happening, even in the most remote places on the planet.

In 2001 I had the distinct privilege of meeting with Mr. Steve Case's leadership team in their corporate offices. Steve Case is the co-founder of America Online. In the year of 2000, Steve was the visionary leader who, with the merger of Time-Warner and America Online, connected the Internet with traditional, mainstream business. When this phenomenal merger took place there was no more doubt in the corporate world that the Internet would forever play a global role in commerce.

Mr. Case's team was more than gracious to allow us to spend half a day engaging in conversation regarding the present and future projections of the Internet. As we were preparing to launch our online platform, we were determined to meet with the best and brightest minds of that era in order to develop the most positive life-engaging platform for the Body of Christ.

The Internet is defined as the worldwide interconnection of individual networks operated by government, industry, academia, and private parties. Originally the Internet served to interconnect laboratories engaged in government research. Since 1994 it has been expanded to serve billions of users and an amazing multitude of purposes in all parts of the world.

The Internet is defined as the worldwide interconnection of individual networks operated by government, industry, academia, and private parties.

In just a matter of twenty years the Internet consolidated itself as a very powerful platform that has forever changed the way modern societies do business and the way we communicate. The Internet, as no other communication medium, has given an international, or if you prefer, a "globalized" dimension to the world. The Internet has become the universal source of information for billions of people at home, at school, and at work.

The Internet is expanding and changing all the time. Two of the most recent phenomenas that have marked the Internet have been the development of social media and mobile technology. These two new innovations have radically and dramatically changed the way people use and interface with the Internet. The social Web people have found a new way to communicate. Since its creation in 2004, Facebook has grown into a worldwide network of over one billion subscribers. In ten years Facebook has gone from one user to one billion! Mobile technology, on the other hand, has made possible a much greater reach of the Internet, increasing the number of Internet users everywhere.

What is amazing today is that new Internet subscribers may not have running water in their home but have lightning speed technology on their mobile phone device. In other words, when I began to use the Internet, as previously indicated above, I began with the turtle-pace speed of 36K to 56K. Yet today ordinary people begin with high-speed Internet via a mobile phone device.

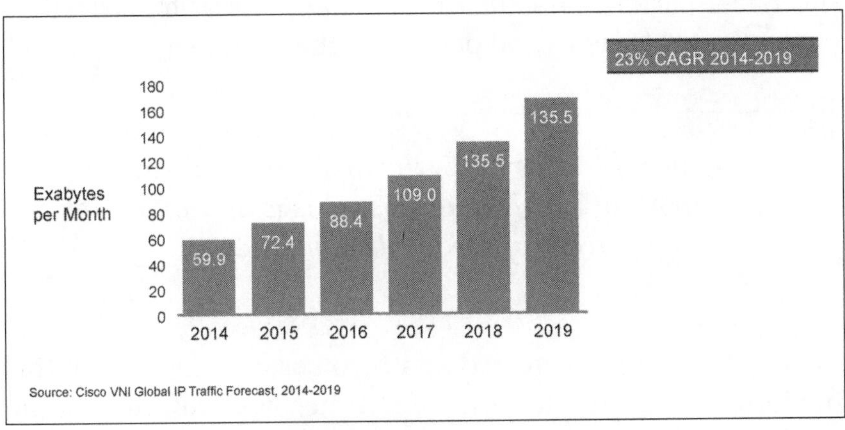

The Internet continues to be the most democratic of all mass media in the world. With a very low investment, anyone can create a Web page on the Internet. This way almost any business can reach a very large market directly, fast, and economically, no matter the size or the location of the business on the planet.

Over a span of fifty years, from 1945 to 1995, the Internet gradually became a reality. In 1962 Leonard Kleinrock invented a packet-switching technology that made the Internet possible for today. The first commercial book about the Internet was published in 1992. It was written by Ed Krol and its attractive title was *The Whole Internet User's Guide and Catalog*.

In January 1955, O'Reilly & Associates, in collaboration with Spry, Inc., announces "Internet in a Box," a product to bring the Web into homes. In February 1955 the World Wide Web was the main reason for the theme of the G7 meeting hosted by the European Commission in the European Parliament buildings in Brussels, Belgium.

At the end of December 1995 there were approximately 16 million users of the Internet. This was 0.4 percent of the world population. As of September 2015, the Internet usage was approximately 3.7 billion users. This is approximately 50 percent of the world's population. In other words, in twenty short, fast-paced years, the Internet has gone from basically 0 percent users to nearly 50 percent of the world's population.[1]

As of September 2015, the Internet usage was approximately 3.7 billion users. This is approximately 50 percent of the world's population.

What does that have to do with you and me? How can this medium be applied to your life? When we were launching the Billion Soul Network at the turn of this millennium, the Internet was picking up speed, from the speed of walking to jogging in metaphorical terms. When I stood before five thousand pastors and leaders at First Baptist Church in Orlando, Florida in 2002, I cast an Internet vision for the future. We articulated that in the future the Internet would catapult more information per year than all of the books that would be required to go from the earth to the sun.

Was this prediction accurate? How much information is catapulted at the speed of light each month and each year on the Internet? The annual growth of the Internet will pass the zettabyte (1,000 exabytes) threshold by the end of 2016 and

[1] "Internet Growth Rates: Today's Road to e-Commerce and Global Trade Internet Technology Reports," Internet Word Stats, http://www.internetworldstats.com/emarketing.htm.

will reach to zettabytes by the end of 2019. By 2016 global traffic will reach 1.0 zettabytes per year, or 88.4 exabytes (nearly 1,000,000,000 gigabytes per month), and by 2019, global Internet traffic will reach 2.0 zettabytes per year or 168 exabytes per month.[2]

Let's look at this information this way:

Bytes (8 Bits)

- 0.1 Bytes: A binary decision
- 1 Byte: A single character
- 10 Bytes: A single word
- 100 Bytes: A telegram

Kilobyte (1,000 Bytes)

- 1 Kilobyte: A very short story
- 2 Kilobytes: A typewritten page
- 100 Kilobytes: A low-resolution photograph

Megabyte (1,000,000 Bytes)

- 1 Megabyte: A small novel OR a 3.5-inch floppy disk
- 2 Megabytes: A high-resolution photograph
- 5 Megabytes: The complete works of Shakespeare OR thirty seconds of a TV-quality video
- 50 Megabytes: A digital mammogram
- 100 Megabytes: One meter of shelved books

Gigabyte (1,000,000,000 Bytes)

- 1 Gigabyte: A pickup truck filled with paper OR a symphony in high-fidelity sound OR a movie at TV quality

---

[2] "The Zettabyte Era—Trends & Analysis," Cisco Systems, May 2015, http://www.cisco.com/c/en/us/solutions/collateral/service-provider/visual-networking-index-vni/VNI_Hyperconnectivity_WP.html.

- 2 Gigabytes: Twenty meters of shelved books OR a stack of nine-track tapes
- 20 Gigabytes: A good collection of the works of Beethoven

Terabyte (1,000,000,000,000 Bytes)

- 1 Terabyte: All the X-ray films in a large technological hospital OR 50,000 trees made into paper and printed
- 2 Terabytes: An academic research library
- 10 Terabytes: The printed collection of the US Library of Congress
- 50 Terabytes: The contents of a large mass storage system

Petabyte (1,000,000,000,000,000 Bytes)

- 2 Petabytes: All US academic research libraries
- 20 Petabytes: Production of all hard disk drives in 1995
- 200 Petabytes: All printed material in 1995

Exabyte (1,000,000,000,000,000,000 Bytes)

- 5 Exabytes: All words ever spoken by human beings

Zettabyte (1,000,000,000,000,000,000,000 Bytes)

- In 2007 this is the informational equivalent to every person on earth receiving 174 newspapers per day.[3]

Did our Internet prediction of 2002 come to pass? Yes! More information is being transported around the world each year than the sum total of all the books stacked on top of each other from the earth to the sun!

[3] Hilbert Martin and Priscilla Lopez, "The World's Technological Capacity to Store, Communicate, and Compute Information." *University of Vermont*, Vol. 332, no. 6025 (February 2010): 60-65.

We chose to ride the information tidal wave across the earth instead of being destroyed on the beach of time. In those early years while the Internet was exploding, we reached out to Dr. John Corts to join our leadership team. For twenty-five years Dr. Corts served as the president of the Billy Graham Evangelistic Association. He has been the "brains" behind the design of the courses and how they would be deployed to the Body of Christ. Each Global Church Learning Center (GCLC) course is comprised of fifteen lessons averaging six to seven minutes per lesson.

More information is being transported around the world each year than the sum total of all the books stacked on top of each other from the earth to the sun!

At the same time, we reached out to Dr. Elmer Towns to serve as the dean of the Global Church Learning Center. Dr. Towns has authored more than 224 books, taught in every world region, and is the co-founder of Liberty University. His educational expertise spans more than sixty years. Through the combined intellect and practical wisdom of Dr. Corts and Dr. Towns, we have been able to birth, build, and broaden one of the finest learning platforms in the global Church today!

After the relational capital had been invested and built, we launched the Global Church Learning Center (www.GCLC.tv). As we highlighted earlier in this book, Christianity is expanding rapidly. Four percent of Christianity is in North America and 96 percent of Christianity is everywhere else. Therefore no matter where we live in the world we know very little about Christianity. It is important for us to learn from men and women from around the globe to obtain a more accurate comprehension of what the Lord is doing worldwide.

For example, if you live in the nation of India of 60 million Christians, this is about 4 percent of global Christianity and 96 percent of Christianity does not live in your nation. If you live in China there are 108 million Christians there. Thus, your nation would be at 8 percent of Global Christianity, but 92 percent of Christianity is not there.

The Global Church Learning Center helps us to learn from the circumference of Christianity at an economical and time-sensitive method for compounding impact for years to come. If you are not a member of the Global Church Learning Center, then go to www.GCLC.tv and sign up today!

The GCLC is not about a single major stream of Christianity, but the entirety of Christianity. As we built this dynamic learning platform, we made some assumptions for this particular environment:

- Every minister needs timely resources.
- Every minister needs to be able to read.
- Every minister needs a core curriculum.
- Every minister needs higher levels of understanding.
- Every minister needs different levels of difficulty.
- Every minister needs flexible sequencing.

- Every minister needs progressive ability, moving the basics to the more complex.

All of the courses were built with certain foundational assumptions in mind. When we think about the five major categories of the Global Church Learning Center (Leadership Development, Global Missions, Church Multiplication, Evangelism & Discipleship, Visionary Networking), each course was designed and deployed to make them as user-friendly as possible.

When a person enters into the Global Church Classroom, he or she will see the top-forty core courses followed by more than one hundred elective courses. Each of these courses have been established with levels of progression in mind, just like a university would arrange them. Once a pastor or leader has completed a certificate, he or she can print this finished certificate on their local office printer and hang it on their office wall!

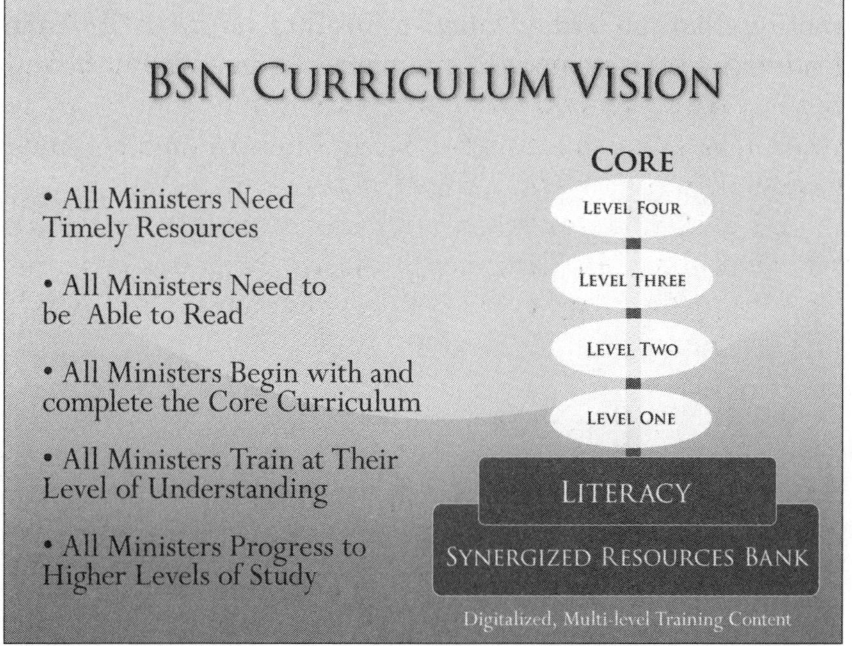

In addition to the Global Church Classroom is the Global Church Library. The Global Church Library is comprised of books, articles, videos, and audios. All of this powerful content is also connected to the courses in the Global Church Classroom. In the years ahead, thousands of additional books and various resources will be added to the Global Church Library for the Body of Christ to utilize for their respective ministries.

In addition to the Global Church Classroom is the Global Church Library. The Global Church Library is comprised of books, articles, videos, and audios.

If you have not chosen to become a member of the Global Church Learning Center yet, I would like to take this opportunity to challenge you to sign up! We receive amazing testimonies from pastors and leaders as to how much they have grown in their personal and professional lives. We believe there will come a day when more than 100,000 Christian leaders are taking courses from every nation in the world!

6

Synergizing for Your Future Success

Speaking the truth in love, we are to grow up in all aspects into Him who is the head, even Christ, from whom the whole body, being fitted and held together by what every joint supplies, according to the proper working of each individual part, causes the growth of the body for the building of itself in love.
—Ephesians 4:15-16

In 1995 when I was going through a bookstore in northwest Arkansas, I saw a book entitled *The Seven Habits of Highly Effective People* by Stephen Covey. I picked up a copy and in that one afternoon read the entire book. Over the years when someone has asked me to recommend a single book I have consistently pointed him to *The Seven Habits of Highly Effective People.*

Stephen Covey, though not a Christ-follower (and I have prayed often for him to come to Christ), hit on powerful elements of real effectiveness. The reader of his book will find that one of the major habits of effective people is the practice of *synergy.* That was the very first time I was introduced to an understanding of the term. Synergy is not a business term; it is a New Testament term. Unfortunately the Church world has from time to time allowed the business community to more effectively grasp a biblical concept which we should be using.

Synergy has been one of those concepts. It comes from the Greek word *synergo,* and it simply means that the whole is greater than its individual parts. When two people come together, they can accomplish significant things that either one could never do by himself. The same is also true when two or three organizations come together and decide they're going to achieve things that they could never do by themselves. *Synergo* is a powerful word!

Over the years I have come to understand that you really can't have a net that works without synergy. You can't achieve significant things far beyond your imagination without each of the team members understanding that he or she has a role in the goal, a part in the heart, and a mission in the vision. Until the team understands the overarching concepts of synergy, they will not figure out ways to add value to one another.

It is not possible to build a net that works without synergy among the leaders.

It seems like just yesterday that I first understood that concept. A number of years ago we began the biennial Synergize Pastors' Conference. We chose the word "synergize" because it really is the epitome of what the Billion Soul Network is all about. We believe that every man and woman has a value to bring into the body of Christ. We believe that the whole body is made up of the whole body. No one is better than the other group, and no one is above or lesser than his or her brother in Jesus Christ.

In the early years of the Billion Soul Network, Dr. Paul Walker, former general overseer of the Church of God and assistant general overseer and leading light in Christianity, really helped us to form the spine of the Billion Soul Network.

In Dallas, Texas, in 2005, a group of men and women met together. During that meeting we fashioned the five elements or the spine of the Billion Soul Network.

The first element is the *sharing of relationships*. We have built the network with the understanding that one of our objectives is to introduce people to one another. It's been amazing to see outcomes that developed after men and women met one another for the very first time. Additionally to that spine of the network, not only did we have relationships, but we also had *resources, reports, recommendations, and reassessment.* So we had the spine that we have built over the years which continues to be comprised of the same five elements that we applied at the very beginning.

There is something very unique and powerful regarding relationship with another man or woman. We often teach that I will treat your friend that you introduced to me the same way that I treat my friend as I introduced him or her to you. It's a powerful force when we are trading on another person's relationship. We often do not realize how much energy, time, blood, sweat, and tears took place for that friendship to be developed. If we're not careful, we mistreat it or we do not treat it with the value at which it should be treated. The shortest distance between two points is not a straight line, but a close relationship. A close relationship that has been developed over time collapses any distance at all.

I believe if we're going to synergize our way to success, there are several steps we need to take in order to achieve this. First of all, we need to *reassess our lives*. We need to take some time to think about what we hope to accomplish in Jesus' name in the next five, ten, or twenty years. Yet this is not the same thing as setting personal goals as much as it is to reach beyond ourselves and find our part in fulfilling the Great Commission. I realize for some the term Great Commission may sound old, but I reassure you, that it truly is the main mission of the Church. It is also to make disciples. It is to tell this whole world who Jesus Christ is.

I would encourage you to reassess every aspect of your life relating to that. If there are some committees that are not helping toward it, get off those committees. If there are some distractions that keep you back, then refocus your life. I encourage you to reassess your life and be willing to lay it on the altar before the Lord. Whatever it is that will be holding you back, be willing to let it go and move forward.

The shortest distance between two points is not a straight line, but a close relationship.

The second step is to *realize there is more*. Make up your mind that you are going to get in sync with what the Lord is doing around the world. Research on the Internet; read books regarding this matter. Not too long ago Dr. Leonard Sweet and I developed a book and released it entitled, *We Are the Church: The Untold Story of God's Global Awakening*. Get a copy of it and, after a few hours, you'll know more about what the Lord is doing than ninety percent of the people living in the West. As you learn that there is so much more than you knew before, determine that you're going to get connected with where the Lord is going today. If you want to know what the Lord is raising up, just look what He has brought to the forefront and you'll know what He's raising up, and you will also know what He's up to.

Thirdly, after you have taken the time to reassess your life and to realize there is more, then begin to *realign your mission*. This realignment will take you some time. Do not try to realign your life and change everything that you've been doing in just a few short months. Realign in your missions giving. Realign in your missions trips. Realign in how you

Early Breakfast Meetings 2002

The Global Stage of
The Billion Soul Network

Bill Bright & James Davis 2001

Billion Soul Network Launch with
5,100 in Attendance 2002

Mel Gibson Interview 2004

Billion Soul Summit with
6,200 in Attendance 2004

Elmer Towns, Jerry Falwell &
James Davis 2005

Mayor Rudy Giuliani
& James Davis

Billion Soul Summit
Johannesburg, South Africa 2005

Billion Soul Initiative Launch
Dallas, Texas 2005

James Davis &
Robert Schuller 2005

Christopher Columbus 2006

The Davis Family with
Chuck Norris

Billion Soul Challenge
Palm Beach, Florida 2005

Last Picture of
Adrian Rogers 2006

Synergize Conference 2006

Billion Soul Summit
Peru 2006

Sir Edmund Hillary &
James Davis 2007

Billion Soul Summit
South America 2007

Oceania Billion Soul Summit
Fiji 2007

Brian & Bobbie Houston,
James Davis 2008

Eurasia Billion Soul Summit
Ukraine 2007

Billion Soul Summit
New Zealand 2008

East Asia Billion Soul Summit
Philippines 2008

East Africa Billion Soul Summit
Kenya 2008

James Davis & Marcus Lamb

Baltics Billion Soul Summit
Latvia 2008

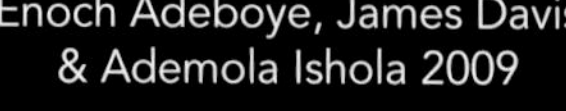

Enoch Adeboye, James Davis
& Ademola Ishola 2009

Leonard Sweet, James Davis,
Kenneth Ulmer 2008

India Billion Soul Summit 2009
David Mohan & James Davis

Richard DeVos, John Sorensen & James Davis

Global Planning for HUBS

Philippines Global HUB Launch Manila, Philippines 2012

Global Church Listening Forum at Foursquare Headquarters 2013

Billion Soul 10th Birthday

Mountains of Ministry 2012

Jack Hayford & James Davis Book Launch

Thomas Trask, James Davis, Reinhard Bonnke

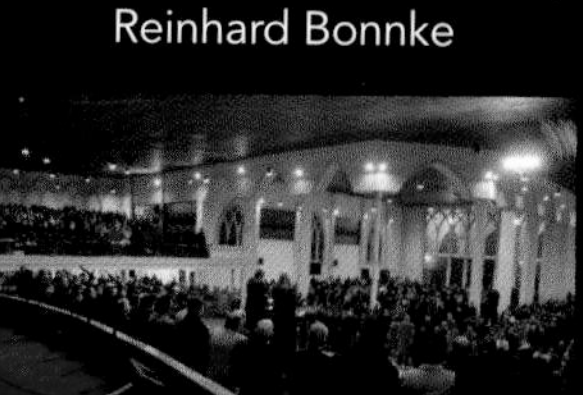

Billion Soul Summit Uganda 2009

James Davis, George Wooc & James Hudson Taylor IV

Oceania Global HUB Launch Fiji 2013

Mark Burnett, Roma Downey & The Davis Family 2014

Global HUB Planning Task Force,
Top of Jungraujoch Summit,
Switzerland 2013

The Davis Family 2014

Indonesia HUB Launch
Surabaya, Indonesia 2014

35th Anniversary of Evangelistic Ministry 2014

Northern India HUB Launch
Delhi, India 2014

Panama HUB Launch
Panama City, Panama 2014

Elmer Towns & James Davis
at 35th Anniversary

Southern India HUB Launch
Chennai, India 2014

The Holy Land 2014

Colombia HUB Launch
Bogota, Colombia 2015

Amsterdam HUB Launch Speakers
Amsterdam, Holland 2015

preach, teach, and lead your people in these matters. Realign as it relates to partnerships, networks, and future synergies that could be part of who you are. I promise you, you will find that you will have a greater fulfillment as a result of it.

Fourth, *recommit to follow through*. So many people begin with wonderful plans but they never finish them. So many people have great ideas, but they never execute them. Many people dream the big dreams but they never develop the teams to make them work. Find a way to see it through and I can promise you, the satisfaction you will have will be more than you've ever imagined in your life.

Be sure to take the time to assess the people that are around you. You need to make sure you're always serving with sheep and not with some wolves that are dressed up like sheep. The years of 2007 and 2008 were two of the most difficult years for me and the Billion Soul Network. There were a few wolves dressed up like sheep that were not interested in networking. They were more interested in not working. In fact, they were more interested in eliminating the ministry than in seeing the ministry flourish.

This was a dark twenty-four-month period of time. I won't take the time to explain it all, but I can say that the words Jesus said on one particular occasion reverberate in my mind. Jesus said there will be those who will say, "Lord, did I not do this? And Lord, did I not do that?" And Jesus will say, "I never knew you." It was said in the context of people who were doing works in the name of Jesus, and yet they did not even know personally in their heart who Jesus was.

The way to bring discernment regarding this matter is to give this man or woman a small assignment. If they're not faithful in a little, do not trust them with much. Then give some more, and then some more, and see if they pass the test. Ultimately what you're looking for in this context is any hidden agenda that is not congruent with the mission and purpose of your network. If that is true, then you need to make up your mind that you're not going to partner with this person or those particular kinds of people. I wish I had learned that lesson early on. It would have saved me much grief, much turmoil, many tears, and also much money. Yet we grow from these things and move on.

I would like to encourage you to take the time to develop a universe of friends—real friends who love you and love the work of the Lord—and spend time sowing and cultivating into those friendships. Those friendships will pay dividends that you could never measure on a scale or in a bank account. Favor is better than labor. Friends are better than almost anything we could ever imagine in this world.

You need to make sure you're always serving with sheep and not with some wolves that are dressed up like sheep.

There are numerous examples of modern synergy that come to mind over the years. There is an pastor friend of mine who has built a phenomenal church in the northern part of the United States. I have been fortunate to minister with him at his church on numerous occasions.

One particular occasion, we talked about unreached people groups. It was during this conversation that he decided he wanted to make a ten percent shift in his thinking, his giving, and his future planning. As we continued to progress in our planning, it came time for us to secure airline tickets for a future trip together. It was during this time I learned he did not like flying at all but he pressed on by bringing a business friend with him on the journey.

We arrived at our destination to advance the Billion Soul Summit. During the strategic conversations that were taking place for the region, it was decided that a interdenominational training center needed to be built in this particular area. When the training center was mentioned, this leading pastor said he would challenge his church to build it in the years ahead.

In the coming years, I watched this pastor continue to make the necessary shifts in his planning for synergistic success. Since that time, he has raised tens of thousands of dollars for reaching people groups that have never heard the Gospel, and has raised up missionaries out of his church and empowered them to relocate to this region!

On another occasion I had a conversation with a pastor who has planted a remarkable church on the eastern seaboard. We talked about unreached people groups and the fulfillment of the Great Commission.

His heart was greatly moved, and his vision clearly extended to a particular region of the world. In this particular region, less than one percent of the people have ever heard the Gospel. Since that time until today, this visionary pastor has raised more than $100,000 for the translation of Scripture, church planting in the region, and for disciple-making. Additionally, he has mobilized his people and has brought a clear-cut focus that one of the strategic reasons his church exists in the world today is for the fulfillment of the Great Commission.

There are many more powerful examples that could be shared to further illustrate the power of synergy. Yet, the overarching point to be made is that if we are ever going to achieve something larger than ourselves, we will have to find strategic and synergistic methods that respect the differences found in our fellow servants and give opportunity for us to "fit together" into a whole body of Christ.

7

Becoming a Reproductive Leader

The things which you have heard from me in the presence of many witnesses, entrust these to faithful men who will be able to teach others also.
—2 Timothy 2:2

At the beginning of this century, I was teaching college courses on "The Telecosm and The Internet World." This was the time period when telecommunications and the Internet were just beginning to join seismic forces that would completely transform our world. As I continued to do research in this dynamic subject and was preparing to launch the Billion Soul Network, I learned "Moore's Law." Moore's law is the observation, that over the history of computing, the number of transistors in a dense integrated circuit doubles approximately every eighteen to twenty-four months. In addition to the doubling of the capacity and speed of the computer, the size of the computer continues to shrink. The law is named after Gordon E. Moore, cofounder of the Intel Corporation, who described the trend in his 1965 paper. Moore's law describes a driving force of technological and social change, productivity, and economic growth in the late twentieth and early twenty-first centuries.[4]

You may ask, "What do telecosm and Moore's Law have to do with 'living the reproductive life?'" I am of the opinion

[4] "Moore's Law," accessed October 25, 2014, *Wikipedia*, http://en.wikipedia.org/wiki/Moore's_law.

that for any sizable societal transformation to occur, there will need to be the doubling of our energy, not just our efforts. No doubt you have heard it said, "We move work smarter; not just harder." Yet, I suggest we take it one step further and implement the reproductive leadership.

If you are not a lover of winning the lost, then you probably have not been won by the Lord. God had only one Son, and He was a foreign missionary. Jesus left a holy place to come to a hellish place; He left a blessed place to come to a broken place; He left a sanctified place to come to a sinful place; He left his crown in heaven to be lifted up on a cross on Calvary's hill.

The light turned green at the cross for everyone to have the opportunity to go to heaven and to live forever.

Jesus died the way He lived. In the Gospel narratives, Jesus lived with sinners and saints. On Calvary, He hung between two thieves. The one on the right received Him and the one on the left rejected Him. Jesus became the "link" between those who choose righteousness and those who choose unrighteousness. The cross became the greatest moral intersection of all time. It is at the cross where people turn right to heaven or left to hell. The light turned green at the cross for everyone to have the opportunity to go to heaven and to live forever.

As Jesus Christ was about to ascend to heaven, He pronounced the Great Commission (Matthew 28:18-20; Mark 16:15-18). He commissioned His disciples to evangelize the whole world. They were not called upon to make decisions, but disciples. Their accomplishments were not to be measured by "counting," but by "conversions." In the first century, the New Testament Church evangelized their world for Christ.

In chapters eight through ten of the book of Acts, the Great Commission is completed by the early Church. These three chapters form a unit on evangelism. They are a trilogy in missiology. In these chapters, the theme is grace for every race. If the contemporary Church is to evangelize the world today, then there are five indisputable truths that must be acknowledged and applied in our evangelism efforts.

First, the reproductive life means that we acknowledge there is a *universal sinner*. In chapters eight through ten of the book of Acts, there were three men who had the same core problem in their lives. They were from different places and distinct races. The Ethiopian eunuch was from Africa. Saul was from Tarsus in Palestine. Cornelius was an Italian from Caesarea. Their common problem was their human depravity or sinful nature.

Every person is born in sin and is therefore a sinner. For example, people are not thieves because they steal. They steal because they are thieves. A corrupted character is the core of the problem in a person's life. The root of the problem is not a racist society, lack of education, financial insecurity, glandular dysfunction, or psychic disorder, but the sinful nature of people. This is basic to effective evangelism. Our foundation must precede our function in evangelism. It is grace for every race.

Second, the reproductive life realizes that there is a *universal seeker*. In these chapters, the Ethiopian, Saul, and Cornelius wanted to know the "truth." They were looking for truth in three different ways. The Ethiopian read the Scriptures (Acts 8:28-31). Saul resisted the Savior (Acts 9:4-5). Cornelius reached out in supplication (Acts 10:2).

People are looking for the truth and meaning to life in different ways today. Many are turning to vices instead of virtues and to cults instead of Christ. The Gospel must be communicated in such a manner so that they can comprehend the elements of salvation and enter into eternal life. Even though on the surface of people's lives, like Saul of Tarsus, there is anger, resentment, and hostility toward the Gospel, we must remember that if God can save us, then He can save anybody. God can take the world's worst sinner like Saul and turn him into the world's greatest Christian. It is grace for every race.

People need to understand that they are not saved through "works" by "faith" in Christ, but by faith in Christ that works! It is grace for every race.

Third, the reproductive life is convinced that there is a *universal Savior*. In chapters eight through ten of the book of Acts, Phillip, Ananias, and Peter preached Jesus Christ to the Ethiopian, Saul, and Cornelius, respectively (8:35; 9:5; 10:36). Jesus is the central theme of evangelism. Methods of presentation may need to change, but the message stays the same forever. There are many ways to happiness, but only one way to holiness. Holiness is not the way to Christ, but Christ is the way to holiness. Christ changes one's character. People need to understand that they are not saved through "works" by "faith" in Christ, but by faith in Christ that works! It is grace for every race.

Fourth, the reproductive life believes in a *universal salvation*. When we share Christ through personal soul winning or in local church crusades, people are going to experience salvation. In the book of Acts, the Ethiopian, Saul, and Cornelius experienced salvation through Jesus Christ (8:37; 9:6; 10:44). Even though they were in different places and from distinct races, God's grace changed their lives forever.

God does not have to go someplace to get to somewhere. He is everywhere at the same time. Whether someone is from America or Australia, South Africa or South America, Mexico or Morocco, Russia or Romania, Cuba or China, Tokyo or Tupelo, God's grace is available in every place and to every race. The American Church must remember that even though our forefathers came to this country on different ships, we are all in the same boat now. We must learn to work together toward effective evangelism.

Fifth, the reproductive life is reminded of a *universal subpoena*. In chapters eight through ten of the book of Acts, there was only one command issued to Phillip, Ananias, and Peter. This command was to "arise and go" (8:26; 9:11; 10:19-20). We must remember that Christ not only said, "Come unto Me," but also, "Arise and go." Someone has noticed that one cannot spell good, God, or Gospel without the word "go." We have been commanded to proclaim Christ to the nations.

It is interesting to further note that Philip, Ananias, and Peter represented different levels of leadership in the New Testament Church. Philip was first a deacon who later became an evangelist. Ananias was a layman. Peter was a Pentecostal preacher. All deacons, laypeople, and preachers are to be soul winners. Regardless of the level of leadership in the local church, the command is to "arise and go." Are you a soul winner? Do you share Christ with unsaved friends? Do you firmly believe that God's grace is for every race? Do you harbor prejudice toward different races? When was the last time you told some lost person about the saving power of Christ? Have you ever won anyone to Christ?

Dr. James Stewart, a distinguished professor of New Testament at the University of Edinburgh, was absolutely correct when he stated, "The greatest threat to Christianity is not communism, atheism, materialism, or humanism, but Christians trying to sneak into heaven incognito without ever sharing their faith and becoming involved in the most significant work God is doing on earth." There are more people alive today on earth than have ever died in the history of the world. If the contemporary Church does not evangelize this generation, then the Church will fossilize in the next generation. If we do not grow and go, then we will dry and die. There are no other options for the Church.

During the Christmas holidays at the close of 2009, I found myself praying, as I so often do at the end of the year, "Lord, help me to be more productive next year than last year." I couldn't tell you how many years I have prayed that.

If the contemporary Church does not evangelize this generation, then the Church will fossilize in the next generation.

However, during this particular Christmas as I was praying, I felt the Lord whisper back to me, "Do not ask Me to make you productive anymore. Begin to ask Me to make you reproductive." Then the Lord went on to add another caveat. He said, "And do not produce anything else that's not worthy of reproduction." When I received that word from the Lord, I felt like He was saying to me, "It is time to get very serious about reproducing and not even waste any time in producing something that's not worthy of reproduction."

All of us have gone to a restaurant from time to time and said, "We're glad this is over because we're never going to come back here again." In reality, if it wasn't worth going the second time, it probably wasn't worth going the first time. I oftentimes challenge pastors and preachers to say, as relates to their sermons, "If it's not worth preaching the second time, it probably wasn't worth preaching the first time." That encourages us to make sure we're constantly doing our best in everything we lay our hands to.

I'm often asked, "Why is the Church reproducing so quickly abroad, and here in the West, we're having such challenges?" I believe one of the answers to that is the essence of simplicity. What we like to do in the West is add more to it, whereas our brothers around the world still keep it fairly simple. I don't mean shallow; I simply mean simple.

It takes eighteen years for an elephant to be able to reproduce and have a second elephant, whereas in that same period of time, rabbits multiply by the thousands. What would you rather be? Would you rather be multiplying at the rate of rabbits, or would you rather be multiplying at the rate of elephants? The answer is obvious.

Paul wrote to Timothy in 2 Timothy 2:2: Train others who might be able to train others also. The whole point of that was to teach what is reproducible so it can be multiplied again. So one becomes two and two becomes four. We all know that it is better to have a penny double every day for thirty-one days than it is to receive a million dollars. We all know at the end of the day that reproduction is the name of the game.

As I have studied movements over a period of time, it is clear that no movement has ever been sustainable without manuscripts. In other words, you have to write. You have to put books together, pamphlets together, booklets together. You have to be able to reproduce your teaching and your training. We live in a day when people say, "Well, I could never write a book," and yet, they text message more than a page a day. Therefore, in a month or two they've done a small book or booklet. Dr. Elmer Towns has often told me to pick up a pen and write every day. Pick up your computer and type every day. If you were to type a page a day, you'd do more than one book a year.

I challenge you to move from production to reproduction. Here are four simple, learnable keys: 1) Listen to leaders carefully; 2) Learn from leaders communicatively; 3) Link with leaders creatively; 4) Lead with leaders consistently. The level and rate by which you are able to reproduce will determine the growth or the speed of growth of your network in the months and years ahead.

8

Networking to Finish Your Assignment

And thus, I aspired to preach the gospel, not where Christ was already named, so that I would not build on another man's foundation.
—Romans 15:20

I grew up in a progressive home where my parents lived full lives and taught their children to think broadly, to work hard, and to believe for the best. As a family we possessed a can-do attitude with a follow-through aptitude. I believe this background prepared me to be ready for open doors and to view the world from many different perspectives.

When I left home in January of 1982 to attend Central Bible College, I had already made some smaller decisions with this philosophy as I viewed my options in light of the bigger picture that the Lord was showing me. Upon arriving at Central Bible College, I was confronted with various world views as well as different understandings of the Church. I remember a conversation with my roommate in which I shared that I planned to preach and minister during my time in Springfield. "You won't be able to do that since there are already so many preachers and pastors in the area," he said. "Oh yes, I will," I responded. "Why are you so confident?" he asked. "Since I'm willing to minister anywhere," I said, "there will always be a place for me to preach and minister."

Herein lies one of the greatest leadership secrets. If we are willing to serve anywhere, there will always be a place for us to serve. This is the kind of outlook needed to see the unseen paradigms that are before us. I have discovered that most pastors genuinely believe they are doing global missions and helping to fulfill the Great Commission in our generation. Yet, their traditional paradigm is not adequate to help them to see what they are not seeing and learn what they are not learning. It took me years before the unseen and the unlearned became seen and learned. I must confess there is still so much more that I do not even know.

In order for us to move from a traditional mission paradigm to a global one, we must first adjust our mind-set. The old school was primarily based on funding and training. The new school is based on networking and partnering. In other words, we have to change our mission's mind-set from parenting to partnering. This is not as easy to achieve as we may first think. As soon as we begin to adjust, we run into missional systems that have been in place for decades and are harder to quickly revise.

For example, if your church has worked from a traditional mission's viewpoint for a long time, you no doubt support a number of missionaries who primarily train and teach the national church in some region of the world. Most likely the majority of these missionaries do not live in unreached people groups of the world. They do not live on the edge of missional endeavors among the unreached, unengaged, people groups of our generation. Dr. James Hudson Taylor IV of Overseas Missionary Fellowship (OMF) teaches the following steps for our moving from parents to partnering.

First, we have to build relationships. There are no shortcuts here. The deeper the relationship, the shorter the distance between the idea and its execution. Second, there has to be mutual ownership. People have to see themselves in the outcome in order for them to go on the long run. Third, effective communication is paramount. Verbal and nonverbal communication must be taken into account. Fourth, we have to leverage diversity and unity. The more we synergize together, the more we can evangelize together.

Often leaders get their first four steps right, but they miss the fifth one. We have to put into place appropriate structures and best practices. If the structures are not right, others will be unable to get plugged into various projects. Sixth, we need motivation for God's glory and the furtherance of His Kingdom. We have to keep the main thing the main thing. I have included a graphic below so you can see how we teach throughout the Billion Soul Network. Once a local church organization begins to make the mental shift from the traditional to global missions, so many more options come into play to achieve the desired outcomes. I must confess I understood some parts of this shift, but the concepts became clearer to me when Reverend Roland Vaughn, former world missions director of the Church of God, taught me this five-point arrowhead.

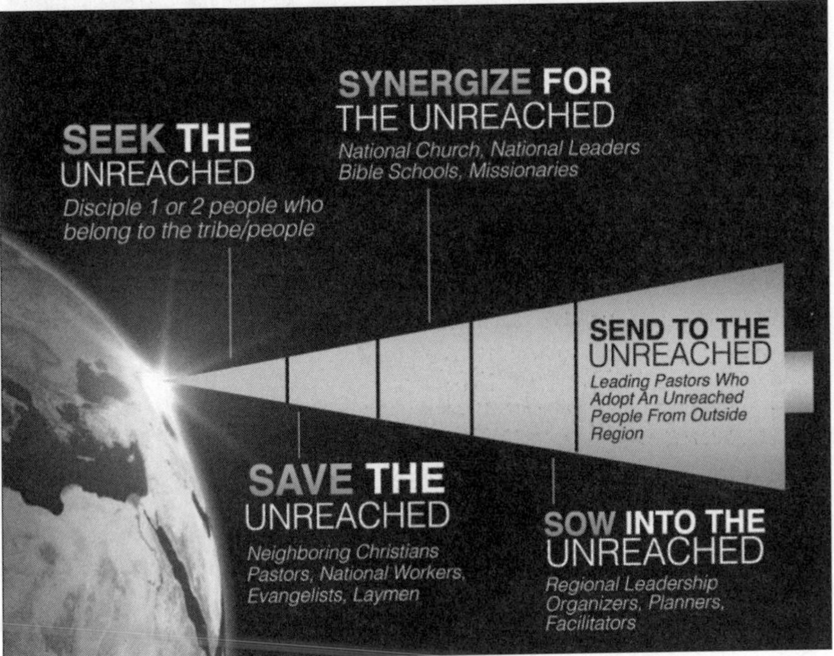

The five points of the missional arrowhead are: seek the unreached, save the unreached, synergize for the unreached, sow in the unreached, and send to the unreached. The five-point arrowhead depicts one of the greatest shifts of missional understanding in our generation. It is my conviction that this network and paradigm will work anywhere in the world. We can see the significant differences between traditional and global missions by viewing them through the lens of the arrowhead.

Traditional missions: here is the five-point arrowhead from the perspective of the traditional mission's practice. Be sure to carefully think through both paradigms, traditional and global, as you strive to move from one to the other. Keep in mind that the global paradigm becomes easier in time as you get to know leaders outside of your silo in various regions on the world.

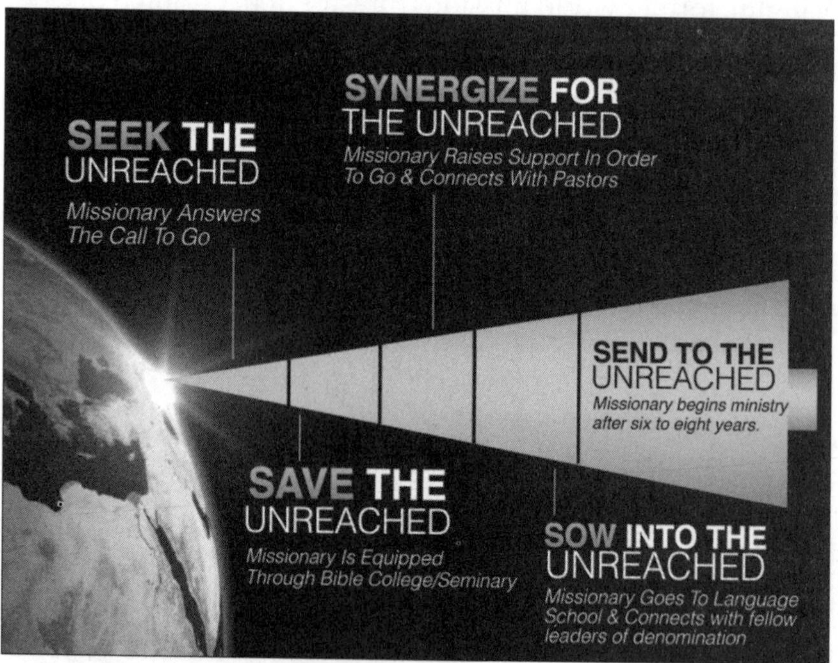

Number One: Seek the Unreached. The missionary answers the call.

Even though I have not officially served as a missionary in the traditional sense, I've served as a missionary in a global sense for decades. Our common understanding is that people as individuals or couples answer the call to be missionaries and connect with their denomination or organization. Oftentimes this calling is first perceived in their youth and fulfilled in the years that follow. The call may be general, it may be focused on a specific country, or at other times the denomination or organization dictates where missionaries will fulfill their God-given calling.

Number Two: Save the Unreached. The missionary is equipped.

For decades the Bible college seminary approach has served the Church with exceptional results. Some mission organizations require up to eight years of training before the missionary can land his feet in a particular world region. Again, while this model has served the Church well for a long time, it faces numerous challenges in the twenty-first century. For example, with the explosion of the Internet, online training is now at the fingertips of anyone in the world.

Number Three: Synergize for the Unreached. The missionary seeks funding.

Once missionaries have gone through a certain amount of schooling, typically the next step is to begin to raise necessary funds to actually go to the called field. This is a grueling task, as they go to the various churches, share their vision, and invite pastors in churches to partner in their effort to provide missions to a particular world region. Depending upon their fundraising skills or how many people they know, this funding phase may take up to two or more years.

Number Four: Sow into the Unreached. The missionary learns the language.

Once missionaries actually get to the field, they have to learn the language and culture in order to do effective ministry. It is not that nothing is done during this phase, but the work is limited until language is grasped enough for effectiveness. Regardless of whether the mission is traditional or global, career missionaries have to learn the language at some point if they plan to stay in the area any length of time.

"Everything the Lord did not tell us to do we have done. But the very thing He told us to do we have not done. He commanded us to finish the Great Commission—that's what we must do."
—Suliasi Kurulo

Number Five: Send to the Unreached. The missionary begins ministry.

Even though the missionaries have been in the field, they are now ready for their assignment and able to begin multiplying ministry. How many years have elapsed since they first entered Bible college's seminary? Think about the answer for a moment. I am not proposing that the traditional approach is inadequate, but that it has been only merely adequate, for the global church was young and not indigenous in so many regions like it is today. What has brought us this far will not by itself get us to the finish line.

Global Missions. I realize that some people will have issues with the terms traditional missions and global missions. In one sense, traditional missions has taken us to global missions, yet going forward, the traditional approach is not going to get us across the finish line of completing the Great Commission. Population growth alone compels us to find more current cutting-edge ways to finish the assignment. In the next ten years, the population of the world will cross eight billion. Suliasi Kurulo of the World Harvest Center in the Fiji Islands says it well, "Everything the Lord did not tell us to do we have done. But the very thing He told us to do we have not done. He commanded us to finish the Great Commission—that's what we must do."

Even though reaching eight billion is just ten years away, we need to strategically plan today what is the best way to reach nine billion people in the next twenty years. Often we strategize how our organization can grow larger next year compared to the past years without giving long-term thought of how our organization can add value to other organizations. Traditional missions help us to grow our own organization; global missions help us to grow our organization along with other organizations for the fulfillment of the Great Commission. Let us envision the arrowhead again, this time through the global networking lens.

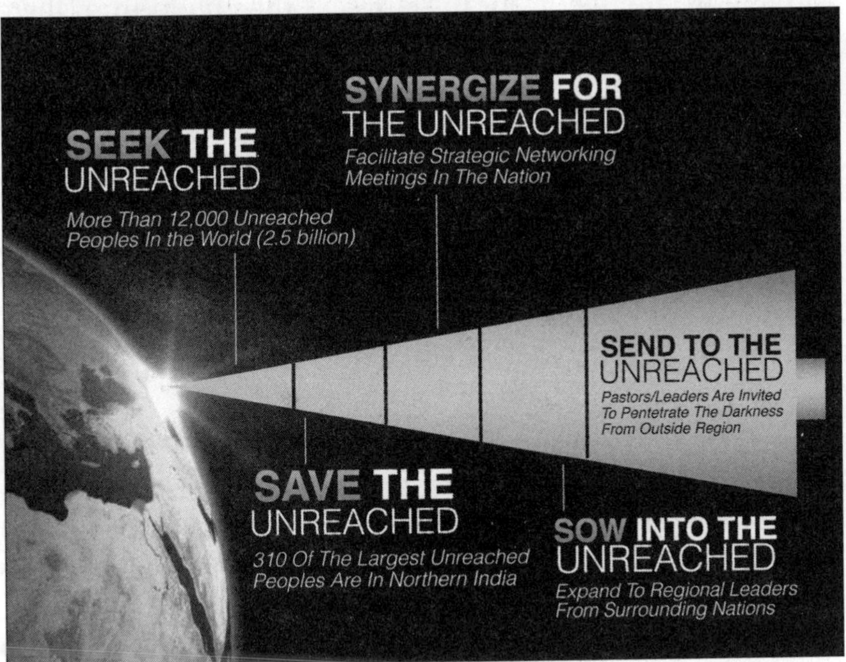

Number One: Seek the Unreached. The missionary networks with one or two disciples who begin with the unreached people group.

We're to begin with a target in mind and work our way from that point. As we've noted, there are more than 16,000 people groups throughout the world. In 1974 at Lausanne, Dr. Billy Graham introduced into missional thinking the concept of people groups, and the significance of that viewpoint has strengthened over the years. The old question was, "How many nations are you in?" The better question is, "How many ethnos or ethnic groups, or people groups are you in?" This is far closer to the original mind-set of the Great Commission spoken by our risen Lord.

Out of 16,000 people groups in the world, approximately six thousand are unreached or unengaged. "Unengaged" means not enough Gospel penetration is taking place to make a significant difference. Pastors and leaders who are targeting these people groups should begin by clearly thinking through where they want to start, and then build from there with the Gospel in mind. We must be thoughtful and intentional, using all resources God has made available, including other Christians. In the past we used to simply answer the missionary call and go without ever thinking about whether or not there were Christians already in the region. Previously there were so few Christians in denominations in these mission fields that it really didn't matter.

The mind-set can be summarized by Dr. Glenn Burris, president of Foursquare Church: "My own concept of unreached people groups was if there was not a Foursquare church, they were unreached no matter who else was there. Today the church has grown up enough to know that the Great Commission is better served when we take the time to ask, who else is already there? If there are one or two disciples who are part of the people group, we can begin our work most effectively by networking with them."

Number Two: Save the Unreached. The missionary networks are Christians who live along the perimeter of the unreached people groups.

Now we are getting somewhere. When we begin to realize the church has grown up, we can begin to move from parenting to partnering. Who else knows better how to get to the unreached people groups than their neighbors? I have witnessed the effectiveness of this approach time and time again in various world regions. In the Billion Soul Network summits, we ask, how do we get from here to there? Who already lives in the region? Who will know what to do and how to do it?

Of course this model can be applied to the unreached in any area of the world. In my opinion, however, of all the dark places on the planet, northern India is the darkest. This is where 310 of the largest unreached, unengaged people groups are found. North of Delhi between Nepal and Pakistan, more than 400 million people live without a witness of the Gospel. Yet over the last twenty years, Dr. Alex Abraham, founder of Operation Agape, has networked to perform an amazing work in this region. I can never imagine going to northern India without first checking in on Alex. He knows his nation "like the back of his hand." Yet the old school of missions is still in session.

Number Three: Synergize for the Unreached. The missionary networks with the national leaders, Bible schools, and missionaries.

I realize there are areas of the world where the Gospel has not penetrated. However, this does not stop us from networking with key leaders who are the closest to the region in order to build bridges in the area. In some nations it's illegal to preach the Gospel. We must build networking bridges if we are ever going to finish the assignment in these regions. In other words, there are hundreds of unreached people groups which each major organization needs to be serving in some way.

For example, India is filled with key leaders from various organizations. Each year Alex Abraham holds a Finish Line Summit where leaders from numerous denominations and organizations come together to connect with key Indian leaders who represent more than 125 unengaged people groups. Over the last five years more than 120 of the unreached people groups have been adopted by key leaders. I cannot imagine a missionary going to India with the old mind-set of working only with "my tribe" to finish the Great Commission.

Number Four: Sow into the Unreached. The missionary networks with others throughout the region.

Now we broaden our minds and ministry to begin to connect with others, even those outside of the target nation, to discover who else is serving in that nation. I believe that the global church is located as it is throughout the earth because our Lord led tens of thousands of leaders throughout the decades to network effectively in order to finish the assignment. In other words, the Gospel is where it is by God's given design. The Holy Spirit has placed various groups in various locations and has called us to connect the dots. He has called us to network to tell the rest of the world about Christ. It is amazing what we learn from other leaders when we choose to seek them out and then sow into their lives.

Number Five: Send to the Unreached. The missionary networks with others outside the region.

As global-minded missionaries, we choose to network even beyond the region of our calling to drive the Gospel into the world's darkest places. Along with networking at the four levels highlighted above, we choose to think even more broadly and bring the global help needed to penetrate the darkness. In the past we just invited pastors to come. Today, we ask, "Who are the best people to come to help us here in addition to the local pastors who are assisting us?"

As we research and network to find others who have similar missional interests and burdens, we gain the knowledge that we need to make wise, concrete decisions. The same Holy Spirit who leads us to specific people groups also directs our paths to others who can come alongside us to work for the greater cause. I am firmly convinced that this five-point arrowhead is the right model for missions as we move forward in the decades ahead. Whether you serve as a pastor or as a leader in an organization, these five steps will work effectively and powerfully for you as you seek the Lord to help fulfill the Great Commission in our lifetime.

The Holy Spirit has placed various groups in various locations and has called us to tie relational knots.

Missions-loving pastor Oswald J. Smith captured the heart of the church with his now-familiar commentary about Christ's miracle of the feeding of the five thousand. Jesus instructed His disciples to seat the people in orderly rows, front to back, Smith explained. When He blessed the bread and broke it, He placed it in the hands of the disciples and they began the task of distribution. They passed along the front rows until everyone had been served; then they went back to the end of the same row and started handing out more bread and fish to the same people. Upon reaching the end of the row, again they turned around and retraced their steps, serving the same people. Is that the way it happened? No, of course not. That would have been wrong. That would have perverted the purpose of the Master. No, they fed everyone, front to back.

Having made that observation, Smith uttered the impactful statement for which he is remembered: "Why should anyone hear the Gospel twice, before everyone has heard it once?"

That challenge confronts today's Church. We have been wonderfully effective in taking the Gospel around the globe, and millions have received the Bread of Life. But millions—literally millions—have not yet heard the message we proclaim.The Church is called today to minister in the vision and spirit of the apostle Paul: "My aim is to evangelize where Christ has not been named…so that those who have not heard will understand."

All of us at one time or another—in a Bible study, in college, or seminary—have studied about the missionary journeys of Paul. We can trace his steps, as he himself stated in the text, from Jerusalem to Albania. He made four journeys, the last one ending in Rome, and then one more journey: the one that ended in heaven in the presence of his Savior. But his dream, his purpose, his passion, his heartbeat—was to reach unreached people. That is the same call that comes, the same vision that inspires Christ's body today.

"Why should anyone hear the Gospel twice, before everyone has heard it once?"
—Oswald J. Smith

One of the principal challenges of the Church today—perhaps THE top priority—is reaching the unreached peoples of the world. The tremendous emphasis we are placing on this vital task of the Church places us precisely in sync with Saint Paul: "My aim is to evangelize where Christ has not been named…so that those who have not heard will understand."

I think enough has been written, enough sermons have been preached, and enough classes and seminars and workshops have been conducted to provide a clear picture of the dimensions of need of unreached peoples. But it is not enough to know the need: We must act on it and take personal ownership.

9

Connecting Your Mountains of Ministry

After these things I looked, and behold, a great multitude which no one could count, from every nation and all tribes and peoples and tongues, standing before the throne and before the Lamb, clothed in white robes, and palm branches were in their hands.
—Revelation 7:9

As you may recall, earlier in this book I highlighted when the Holy Spirit challenged me "to look for what I have raised up" throughout the world. I took that moment in time as an unction from the Lord to travel and to connect personally with key leaders whom the Lord had anointed for their world region. In my heart, the metaphor formed as to what we now call "The Mountains of Ministry." Just like a mountain range that is connected with small, medium, and large mountains from the beginning to the end, the Lord was in essence saying: "I have raised up a mountain range of ministry throughout the world that is interconnected to one another and to Me."

Just like Eliazer did not fully know how he was going to find "the bride" for Isaac, when we begin following the path our Lord has placed before us, we don't fully know how all the necessary pieces will come together to fulfill the goal that our Lord has set before us. Yet, we know in our heart, if we are faithful, we will be successful with our mission.

With this mind, in November 2006, our team was hosting a Billion Soul Summit in Johannesburg, South Africa. We were thrilled with the enormous response of African leaders who chose to join us for this historic gathering. Pastor Ray McCauley, the founding pastor of Rhema Bible Church, hosted us. Toward the close of this summit, Dr. David Sobrepeña, founding pastor of Word of Hope, Manila, Philippines, shared with me the concept of the HUBS as training locations. We both agreed that we should strategically pursue this after the global training was launched throughout the Body of Christ.

Just like a mountain range that is connected with small, medium, and large mountains from the beginning to the end, the Lord was in essence saying: "I have raised up a mountain range of ministry throughout the world that is interconnected to one another and to Me."

The point I want to make here is that when one is building the network, he or she must have an overarching plan and make doubly sure that professional and personal relationships are growing over time. With this in mind, even though we knew the HUB concept was a winner, we still knew we had to develop and deploy the training first. In 2010, Dr. Sobrepeña and I were once again working together in Quito, Equator. We came in a day early ahead of a massive Billion Soul Summit to devote an entire day to the finishing of the training themes and the selection of the HUB locations. When everything was finally set, we launched the first Global HUBS of Christianity at Word of Hope, Manila, Philippines, in March 2012.

Dr. Sobrepeña and I worked together strategically on this first HUB for many months in order to bring about a successful launch. Nearly one thousand pastors and leaders joined us for this historic gathering. We chose to launch the first HUB and the Global Church Learning Center in Asia to make a statement to the global church. Repeatedly we have said that it is no longer the Gospel going from the West to the rest, but the best around the world going to the rest of the world. All of us came from different strains of Christianity but chose to get into the same river of revival today.

The second global HUB of Christianity was launched in Surabaya, Indonesia. We partnered with Pastor Alex Tanuseputra and his world-class team. More than nine thousand pastors and leaders converged together for this remarkable gathering of the body of Christ.

Most of us in the West have no idea of the growing churches in Indonesia. Pastor Tanuseputra's church average is 180,000 on the weekend, and more than two thousand churches have been planted from this church. In the last thirty years there has been a great surge in Christian growth throughout all of Indonesia. At the time of this writing, nearly 25 percent of Indonesia has become Christian. We are most grateful for the key leaders that joined Pastor Alex and me for this second HUB launch.

The third global HUB of Christianity was launched in Suva, Fiji. As I have shared previously in this book, Pastor Kurulo is leading an amazing movement of missionaries and church planters worldwide. More than eight thousand pastors and leaders joined us for this launch of the global HUB of Christianity called Oceania. With this HUB launch, a major part of the billion soul vision was fulfilled. As you may recall, in the early days leaders indicated that we would never be successful in the island nations because the Internet was not there. I am grateful to report that every island nation is represented in the Billion Soul Network, and pastors and leaders are taking courses in the Global Church Learning Center!

Our next global HUB of Christianity was launched in Santiago, Chile. Pastor Castro Duran and I partnered together for this event. The Pentecostal Methodist Church is the very first church to experience Pentecost after the Azusa Street revival in 1909. At the time of this writing, they have had only four pastors since the church formed. For more than one hundred years this remarkable church has experienced sustainable growth year after year. Today, more than 540,000 people call the Pentecostal Methodist Church their home church. Dr. Elmer Towns and I were the keynote speakers for the launch of this global HUB. More than 11,000 pastors and leaders joined us as we committed to train pastors and leaders like never before throughout South America and the world.

The fifth and sixth global HUBS of Christianity were launched in Deli and Chennai, India. In Delhi, approximately eight hundred church planters and leaders convened from north of Deli and between Pakistan and Nepal. It was the largest such gathering ever. More than 130 unreached people groups were represented in this HUB launch.

Dr. Alex Abraham, founder of Operation Agape and cochair of Unreached People Groups, provided phenomenal leadership for this HUB launch. In the last twenty years, through his ministry Dr. Abraham has witnessed more than 15,000 house churches being started in northern India. I consider northern India to be the spiritually darkest place in all the world.

When this HUB launch concluded we quickly jumped on a plane to fly to Chennai, India. Dr. David Mohan, pastor of New Life Assembly of God and cochair of India, greeted us upon our arrival. We were thrilled once again to partner with him and his remarkable team. Over the last forty years, New Life Assembly has grown to nearly 50,000 people and has also helped to plant two thousand more churches in India. At the time of this writing, we are partnering with Dr. Mohan in the planting of more than 20,000 more churches in the next five years! For the southern India HUB launch, approximately 1,200 pastors and leaders joined us from every major stream of Christianity.

The eighth global HUB of Christianity was launched in Panama City, Panama, in October 2014. We had a record attendance with fifteen hundred key pastors and leaders joining us from every Central America nation. Pastor Antonino Garcia is leading an amazing state-of-the-art church in this region. In the years ahead, it is projected that at least ten thousand Christian leaders will go through the Global Church Training Curriculum that will be taught in the Panama City HUB!

It is not that the Bible is no longer pungent or the power of the Holy Spirit resourceful, but it is that we have stepped away from our first love in Christ.

The ninth global HUB of Christianity was launched with nearly 250 pastors and leaders from eighteen nations in Amsterdam, Holland. This was the first Billion Soul Summit scheduled in Europe for the years ahead. The nations represented were: Holland, England, Spain, Germany, Belgium, Monaco, France, Switzerland, Ukraine, Romania, Hungary, Austria, Italy, Canada, United States, Fiji, Philippines, and India.

In addition to the synergistic networking that took place, the formation of two of the Global HUBS of Christianity have emerged in northern and southern Holland. This demonstrates the power of reproduction! A Global HUB synergizes the best relationships, systematizes the best training and strategizes for unreached people groups. The speakers included: Stanley Hofwijks, Holland; Edgar Holder, Holland; David Mohan, India; Suliasi Kurulo, Fiji; James O. Davis, United States; Peter de Leau, Holland; Leon Fontaine, Canada; Martin Mutyebele, Belgium; and David Sobrepeña, Philippines. Many leaders expressed that this was the best European Summit they have attended in many years. Please note carefully how the Billion Soul Network pulls leaders from around the world to focus their efforts on another region of the world.

Over the last thirty years, I have heard people repeatedly say, "When will we see the next great revival in America? Why is it that we see such great moves of God abroad but not very much happening here?" What is the answer? I believe that it is time for the West to learn from the rest and also to experience what they have been witnessing for decades now. It is not that the Bible is no longer pungent or the power of the Holy Spirit resourceful, but it is that we have stepped away from our first love in Christ. We must believe our beliefs and doubt our doubts.

With this in mind, the Billion Soul Network is engaged throughout North America. We were fortunate to launch our first global HUB of Christianity at Green Acres Baptist Church with David Dykes in Tyler, Texas, in November 2014. Our strategic comprehensive master plan calls for thirty-five strategically located HUBS in the United States and another five to seven such HUBS in Canada. We are praying and believing that what the Lord is doing around the world, He will once again do in the United States and Canada. Key leaders from every major stream of Christianity joined us for this HUB launch in Tyler, Texas. On Wednesday night we dedicated this HUB to the Lord with more than one thousand people joining us!

How many HUBS will there be? For approximately two years, key leaders in the Billion Soul Network met to develop an overarching global strategic plan. With this plan came the mathematical goal of one HUB for every ten million people throughout the world. This kind of global metric allows us also to take into account the population growth that is coming before us. For the first time, the global church will be able to make plans according to population growth rather than chasing population! If we are ever going to finish the Great

Official Travel Partner of Billion Soul

Fellowship Travel International • (800) 235-9384 • www.fellowship.com

Custom Faith-Based Tours

Create a trip that is not just spiritually-fulfilling, but completely unique & on budget. You can add a wide variety of: hands-on volunteer, cultural & culinary experiences.

Your FTI Team

Our Tour Agents use their personal experiences traveling the world to design once-in-a-lifetime experiences for each group.

Your Custom Itinerary

Partner with your tour coordinator to create a spiritually-rewarding itinerary that meets your group's goals & budget.

Your Ideal Guide

We have chosen an elite group of guides – the best in the business. And, we'll match you with the one that's just right for you.

Just Pick a Focus

We have a variety of sample itineraries, including additional day tour & stopover options to get your planning started.

Holy Land

New Testament

Old Testament

Choir

Fellowship

Reformation

Official Travel Partner of Billion Soul

Fellowship Travel International • (800) 235-9384 • www.fellowship.com

Mission Travel Experts

Fellowship Travel works with hundreds of mission teams & thousands of individuals each year. With this buying power, we've negotiated special contracts for mission travel with a variety of international carriers.

Benefits can include:

- **Reduced missionary rates**
- **Advanced booking** to lock in low rates (up to 11 months before travel)
- **Refundable deposits** to hold group space
- **Name & date changes**
- **Additional baggage**
- **Flights can originate overseas**

Looking for a New Mission Project?

We can network you with global ministries in need of your specific God-given talents. Ask about projects focused on the topics below or create your own!

Construction

Orphan Care

Disabled Care

Evangelism

Medical

Feeding

Sports

Arts

Commission, we have to get ahead of population growth and tell everybody about the Lord.

What does a HUB do? There are three significant outcomes for the global HUBS of Christianity. First, we are synergizing the best relationships throughout the entire body of Christ. Secondly, we are systematizing the best training and making it available worldwide. Thirdly, we are strategizing through every major stream of Christianity for unreached people groups.

In the next five to seven years, we anticipate more than 75,000 pastors and leaders going through the global HUBS for the purpose of networking to help fulfill the Great Commission in the twenty-first century.

As we wrap up this chapter, we seek to communicate clearly our approach. In order for The Global HUBS of Christianity to be as effective as possible, key leaders in their respective regions are empowered to start additional HUBS where they believe they are best suited and located in their area. We would never ask for a key leader from outside of the US to come to North America and tell us where we should establish our HUBS, and neither will we go to a specific area in the world and tell them where they should locate their HUBS. We believe the neighbors know best where HUBS should be located and who the HUB host should be. By the end of 2016, the projections are that there will be more than eighty global HUBS of Christianity worldwide. This is only the beginning of the reproduction! It is estimated by 2022 there will be at least eight hundred Global HUBS of Christianity!

10

Going After Your Impossible Dream

And without faith, it is impossible to please Him, for he who comes to God must believe that He is and that He is a rewarder of those who seek Him.
—Hebrews 11:6

Three times in Exodus 14, the Word of God instructs us by saying that the Lord led them. Can you honestly say that you want the Lord to lead you? Sometimes the Lord leads us to the mountaintops where the eagles soar and at other times to the valleys where the scorpions roam. Sometimes He leads us to the sunshine and sometimes to the starlight. Can you honestly say that you want God to lead you?

When you choose to go after your impossible dream, there will be some who will go with you and others who will choose not to do so. When God was leading the nation of Israel out of Egyptian bondage, He chose to lead them in unique and powerful ways. This is also the way God chooses to lead us in the twenty-first century. Sometimes the Lord leads us in mysterious ways and sometimes in miraculous ways. Sometimes He leads us in a zigzag line and other times in a straight line. I want you to understand how God leads us.

First of all, **sometimes He leads us on detours.** The Word of God says that God did not lead them the short way, but He led them the long way. He chose not to take them the shortest route through the wilderness on to Canaan. God chose to take them on the long route. Why do you suppose God chose to take them the long way instead of the short way? Well, the Word of God makes it very clear.

God said that if He had led them the short way, they would meet the Philistines, and they would not be ready for war. God knew something about them that they did not know about themselves. Maybe they thought they were ready for the fight of their life, but God knew they weren't ready for it yet. So God took them the long way. It was one thing for the Lord to bring them out of Egypt. It was another thing to get Egypt out of them. In fact, it took Him a lot longer to get Egypt out of them than it was to bring them out of Egypt. So God led them on a detour.

Detours teach you how to walk.
Detours teach you how to handle delays.

Sometimes God leads you on a detour to teach you how to walk. He slows things down. He puts things in your path that you did not see coming. Have you ever been driving on a trip or going through a city and all of a sudden you see a detour sign? Well, your GPS didn't tell you there was a detour ahead, but all of a sudden you realize it's going to take you longer than you thought it was going to take. That's what detours do. Detours teach you how to walk. Detours teach you how to handle delays.

But God does not leave you alone when He leads you on the detour. What did He do for the nation of Israel? He had a cloud in the day and a pillar of fire at night. All they had to do was keep their eyes on the cloud or keep their eyes on the pillar of fire and they would know a sense of timing and the direction to go.

Can you imagine the scene with me? Maybe you're tucking your children into bed and all of a sudden a man opens a tent and says, "It's not time for bed. It's time to get up and get moving," and you may say, "No, we'll do something tomorrow." But the man responds, "But the pillar of fire is moving." So you pack up your children and your belongings and you start following the pillar of fire. Maybe you're having breakfast in the morning and you've just finished giving praise to Jehovah for a new day and all of a sudden the clouds just begin to move. When God gives you a sign, He gives you a sense of timing and He gives you a sense of direction. You don't always have to know where God is going; you just simply have to be following Him every day.

When I was a child in school, just like you, there came a time that I had to learn how to play "follow the leader." We students got in a line and followed the teacher. We didn't know everything there was about the teacher. We didn't even know where the teacher was going, but we followed. When our teacher moved, we moved, and when the teacher stopped, we stopped. We learned how to play follow the leader.

In the last twenty to twenty-five years there has been much written about leadership, but not that much written about "followership." The last time I checked, the Lord is still the leader and we're still the followers. Oftentimes we talk about our leadership more than we talk about our followership. The apostle Paul would say, "Follow me as I follow Christ." He wouldn't simply say, "Follow me and I'll show you the way." It is time for you (and for me and the Church in the twenty-first century) to learn how to follow the Lord.

When the Lord puts us on a detour, He teaches us dependence. He teaches us how to move when He moves and to stop when He stops. These are the lessons of the detour. It's so interesting when you think about it because God lead the nation of Israel into Egypt. God gave them a promise that one day He would bring them out, but it would be four hundred years before this process would take place. It was a constant detour to ultimately fulfill the promises that God had made to them in a previous generation.

When you choose to go after your God-given dream you need to understand there are going to be challenges which you didn't anticipate. There are going to be problems you didn't think about. There are going to be people that will try to tear you down or discourage you. You won't be able to plan for them. There will be financial challenges you could not calculate because you are on a path you have not been on before.

It is like driving a car in the night fog. All you can see is the dotted line in front of you. But if you keep your eye on the dotted line and you have a sense of direction, you will ultimately end up at the right place. I'm not recommending that you spend your life driving through the fog, but you need to realize that when you decide you are going to do something that has not been done before, the path will not be carved out for you. Therefore, you have to learn to depend on the Lord to lead you in the daytime and to lead you in the nighttime, to lead you in mysterious ways and to lead you in miraculous ways.

Second, sometimes God leads to dead ends. If you don't enjoy the detours, you're not going to enjoy the dead ends. It's one thing for the Lord to lead us on a detour where life slows down and things get delayed from time to time. But it's another thing for the Lord to intentionally lead us to a dead end. The Bible says in Exodus14 that God led them to the Red Sea. God did that. They were now hemmed in between the sword and the sea. They couldn't go up and around and they couldn't go down and around because there were mountains above the Red Sea and-mountains below the Red Sea. They couldn't go back because Pharaoh and his army in red-hot pursuit behind them. In fact, they couldn't hear the sound of the chariot wheels. They couldn't hear the sound of the armor, and yet they were standing in front of the Red Sea.

It's one thing for the Lord to put us on a detour to teach us how to walk. It's another thing for the Lord to bring us to a dead end to teach us how to walk. When the Lord puts us on a detour, He teaches us how to follow through. But when He brings us to a dead end, He teaches us how to handle fear.

I want you to see what happened when they got there. Here they are standing at the Red Sea, some two million men and women, and the first thing that Moses says is to "fear not." That's almost hilarious to me. God brings them to a fearful place and He tells them not to be afraid. God knows something about human nature. We will never overcome fear until we're willing to face it and walk through it.

When the Lord puts us on a detour, He teaches us how to follow through. But when He brings us to a dead end, He teaches us how to handle fear.

It's like the person who is afraid to get on an airplane. He goes to the airport and watches the planes take off and land, thinking that's going to help him overcome his fear of flying. He won't ever overcome his fear of flying until he gets on that plane and takes off and lands, probably many different times. With this same fear, the nation of Israel has been brought to the brink of disaster. They are standing on the edge of the Red Sea and Moses says, "Be not afraid."

When you choose to go after the impossible dream, you will face fears from time to time: fear of what other people may think, fear of how you would provide for this, fear of the unknown, fear of questions that no one else has asked. Yet you have to be figuring out an answer, a solution that applies to many, and maybe multitudes, and not just to a few.

Not only did Moses say, "Fear not," but then he also said, "Stand still." It's interesting that he told them not to try to solve it, not to try to move, but to stand still. He was teaching them that waiting on God is not wasting time before God. He is also teaching them that if you learn to wait on the Lord He will truly renew your strength. What's interesting about the story is that on this particular evening the pillar of fire is no longer in front of them, but the pillar of fire is behind them. It is God that is protecting His people from Pharaoh and his advancing army. Moses goes on to say that they will never, ever see them again. You see, when we learn to wait on the Lord and allow Him to fight the fight of faith with us and for us, we will never, ever again see the things that we have dreaded, feared, and fretted over the most.

You see, when we learn to wait on the Lord and allow Him to fight the fight of faith with us and for us, we will never, ever again see the things that we have dreaded, feared, and fretted over the most.

Then Moses tells everybody to be quiet. That is one of the hardest things that the nation of Israel could ever do because they liked to talk, murmur, and complain about almost everything. Negativism may spread, but negativism doesn't save. If you want to know what's in a person's heart, just listen to what they talk about all the time and you will know what's in their heart. Moses was teaching the nation of Israel to be still, to be unafraid, to be quiet, and to wait upon the Lord.

Just because an idea comes to your mind doesn't mean you have to say it. Just because a thought crosses your mind doesn't mean you have to express it. It's powerful to pause before you speak and decide whether it's worthy of even uttering. So many people have a self-fulfilling prophecy because they sit around and talk about how bleak things are, and you know what? Usually things become bleak and pretty bad because they turn out to be a self-fulfilling prophecy. You and I are going in the direction of our most dominating thought. We are going in the direction of what propels us forward according to how we think in our lives.

Moses then picks up the rod of God, waves it across the Red Sea, and of course you know the story. God parts the waters, turns a dead end into a four-lane highway, and nearly two million people walk through on dry ground. What is interesting about the story is that the Bible doesn't tell us about the first ones to get into the water. The Bible doesn't make that clear to us, but there were some who took that first step of faith as those waters were parting, wondering if the waters would capsize back on top of them. However, once they took the first step, the others followed.

As you launch out into what God has planned for you, some people will never fully understand the step of faith you took, the sacrifices you made, the position you chose, and the path you followed. All they will enjoy is the parted waters. All they will enjoy is the thing that they can see. But they didn't see what it took in order for it to become a reality. They didn't see the forty years of the wilderness wandering for Moses himself before he announced to Pharaoh that it was time for the people to depart. The Bible says God led them through the Red Sea to the other side, and Pharaoh and his army tried but, of course, were destroyed. The chariot wheels washed on the seashore of the Red Sea, and archaeologists to this day from time to time have found the ancient ruins of Pharaoh and his army from so many centuries ago.

Third, sometimes God leads to dry holes. There are going to be detours and dead ends when you choose to go after what God has for you and the dream that He has put in your heart. You also need to be prepared for the dry holes. When they got on the other side of the Red Sea, Moses was their hero. In fact, the first song in the Bible was written in Exodus chapter 15, and then the last song in the Bible is in the book of Revelation. It's called "The Song of the Lamb," but the first song was all about Moses. Moses was their hero; it was the number one song of the land. Everybody was singing it. It was number one on the charts, but three days later, Moses went from hero to zero.

Three days later nobody was singing the song of Moses. No one was excited ever again to hear the song of Moses. Why? Because they had entered a dry period. They entered into a very difficult and fragmented time in their wilderness wanderings. It's one thing for you to learn how to handle the detours and to walk, the dead ends and to wait, but the dry holes in worship are at a totally different level. When people disappoint you, when things seem to be so bad, or people have walked away, how do you handle those moments in your life? Are you going to get larger, or are you going to get smaller? Are you going to become a connector, or are you going to choose to become a complainer? Are you going to become one filled with faith, or are you going to turn around and go back the other way?

The Word of God says that they have run out of water, and now they are looking everywhere trying to find it. They go to this well, to that well; can you even imagine the disappointment they are experiencing? The disappointment of this dry hole, the disappointment of that dry hole, and the situation has become extremely serious because within a matter of days you can lose a million people with the lack of water. So the people began to murmur and complain. In fact, it gets so bad that in Exodus 16:8, Moses addresses the people and says, "You think your murmuring is to me, but your murmuring is to God."

Whatever is in the well of the heart will come out in the bucket of speech. Just listen to what people like to talk about and you will know what's in their minds and in their hearts. If you're going to enjoy what God has for you, sooner or later you're going to have to realize that even though you are walking through a dry period, God knows how to provide when other people seemingly have turned away and walked back on their commitment.

So, the children of Israel were murmuring and complaining. Do you know what murmuring does? It stifles spiritual growth. Murmuring digs a rut that becomes a grave. Murmuring is what stops people from moving forward. Have you ever spent time with someone you haven't seen in years who is still complaining about the same thing from five or ten years ago? He says things like, "When Betty behaves, I'm going to grow up," or, "When Bob does right, I will move forward," and yet it's not really about Betty or Bob. It's about that person deciding to move forward and move out of what others have chosen to live their lives with.

If you're ever going to fulfill that so-called impossible dream, you're going to have to spend time with the right people, choose your friends carefully, and let go of those who choose to live their lives filled with the most negative expressions.

The Bible says the Israelites are facing a difficult time. They are murmuring, and it was in this situation that God says, "This is enough." He says, "Because of your murmuring I am going to let you die in the wilderness." It was the murmuring that brought them down. It was the complaining to God that ultimately caused them to dig their own graves in the wilderness. Now was this God's plan for their life? No, but God was bringing them through a testing to find out what was inside.

When I got up this morning I squeezed toothpaste, and when I did, toothpaste came out. When life squeezes you, what comes out of you? Is it sour, or is it sweet? Is it pleasant, or is it painful? Is it joyful, or is it the most negative, terrible thing that you could ever express? What comes out of you is so much the picture of what you become or who you have chosen to become, and it was there that God let them die.

When you look in 1 Corinthians chapter six you will find that Paul is writing to the church in Corinth and he says, "Don't be like the Israelites were when they created idols and they worshipped. Don't be like the Israelites were when they tempted God." Then he says, "Don't be like the Israelites were when they committed immorality or adultery," and then he says, "And don't be like the Israelites were when they murmured." He put murmuring in the same bed with immorality, idolatry, and tempting God. If you want to understand who you are, just look at the people in your life and you'll know who you are. We attract who we are, not what we want. If you're ever going to fulfill that so-called impossible dream, you're going to have to spend time with the right people, choose your friends carefully, and let go of those who choose to live their lives filled with the most negative expressions. You're going to have to move forward in what God has for you.

Then Moses sees a river and it's called Marah, because it means bitter. Can you even imagine? The people think they're saved. The people think, "We have found the river. We'll have plenty of water," but when they get there to taste it, it's bitter, and sometimes it's that way. As you're carving your path, as you're going into the unknown, there are things that you will taste and say, "That tastes so bitter to me," and yet the Lord has a way of turning what is bitter into sweet. So Moses takes the limb of a tree, throws it into the river, and the Bible says that the water becomes sweet. Now they have salvation, the two million people have plenty of water, but they're still going to die in the wilderness because they have chosen to live that way.

In order for you to accomplish what God has for you or for me, we have to take the cross of Jesus Christ daily, put it into the fountainhead of our heart, and allow the sweetness to come out in a bitter-filled world. Until we learn this and learn how, as the apostle Paul would say, "to die to self daily," we will never achieve what God has for us. These are the detours that teach us how to walk. These are the dead ends that teach us how to wait. These are the dry holes that teach us how to worship.

Whatever it is that God has put in your heart, pursue it today, and you will see in time that what's in your heart, you will hold in your hand.

What's so amazing as this story comes to a close? The Bible says in Exodus chapter 13 verses 17, 18, and 19 that God gives instructions through Moses for some people to go back in and get the bones of Joseph. The Bible doesn't tell us who it is they choose to go find the box that contains the bones of Joseph, but they go in, find the box, and bring it out of Egypt, and Joseph goes along with the two million people. While they are burying people in the wilderness, Joseph just continues on the journey. He had said that when they leave, "You have to promise that you'll take me with you." They carry him the entire wilderness time of some forty years. They carry him in Canaan for ten to fifteen more years, and finally they bury him in a small town called Shechem. That's the same place that Joseph buried his dad, Jacob, more than one hundred years earlier. It simply means a place of prosperity. It is here that Joseph is buried, in prosperity.

The point is this: what God starts in your life, He will finish in your life. If you stay faithful, one day you will hold in your hands the dream that is put in your heart. You'll be able to say that what God whispered to you in the night has become a reality in the daytime. Don't allow individuals around you to rob you of what God has put in your heart. Determine that you're going to pursue it and stay faithful, and God will provide for you.

I can tell you there have been those times of delay as it relates to the Billion Soul Network. We've had to learn how to walk instead of run. There have been those dead ends where we just did not know what we were going to do next and how we were going to get through a difficulty. There have been dry holes where people have chosen not to follow through, or tried to dismantle or undermine us, but we decided that high ground was better than low ground, that the second mile is better than the first mile, and that we have to pursue and stay faithful until the vision becomes a reality. I want to encourage you to do the same. Whatever it is that God has put in your heart, pursue it today, and you will see in time that what's in your heart, you will hold in your hand.

11

Conquering Life's Greatest Challenge

This is the day that the Lord has made.
We will rejoice and be glad in it.
—Psalm 118:24

I believe as we strive to finish the Great Commission to plant local and global churches, the tyranny of time, the redeeming of time, is the greatest challenge that is before us. Never before have we been busier, and yet we do not have much to show for it. Activity does not necessarily mean accomplishment. Busyness does not necessarily mean business. Decision-making does not necessarily mean discipleship-making.

So what is life's greatest challenge? What is it that keeps us from achieving what we've had two thousand years to do? I would like to summarize it in this simple expression, "Turning every God-given day into a God-governed day so it might become a God-gladdened day." I believe all of us know the verse in Psalm 118 verse 24. It says, "This is the day that the Lord has made. I will rejoice and be glad in it." It is in this single riveted verse that we can face life's greatest challenge and overcome it for God's glory. That's what I want to talk to you about, because I believe once we understand as fellow leaders what the facts are about every day that is given to us, then we can truly maximize the moment, we can strategize the day, and we can leverage it for God's glory.

First, we have a **provided day**. The Bible says, "This is the day that the Lord has made." The Lord has provided each of us with this day. It is not necessarily how many days we might have, but it is the fact that we are given a brand new day. God does not have to take life away from us. He just has to stop giving us another day; and with the lack of another day, life comes to a close.

Each of us has the same amount of time every day, week, month, and year. Each of us has 14,400 minutes and 86,000 seconds in each day. We may have more money than somebody else, but we don't have more minutes than somebody else. The richest person on this planet doesn't have any extra time than you or I have. It is not the amount of time; it is how we use the time that makes all the difference. I have often heard people say, "I just wish I had more time." Well, we all have the same amount of time each day. It is how we choose to use that time that makes all the difference for eternity.

We may have more money than somebody else, but we don't have more minutes than somebody else.

I once read an article about a man who had purchased a seven-million-dollar watch. Can you even imagine a seven-million-dollar watch? I can't even think of what must go into a watch to make it worth seven million dollars. No doubt it was filled with precious stones and was gold filled or gold plated. But even though the man purchased this seven-million-dollar watch, he doesn't have any more time than either you or I have. You see, it really doesn't matter if your watch is seven dollars or seven million dollars; you still only have this day and no more. It is important that we realize that God has provided this day. I have often said that it may only be

TRAINING RESOURCES DESIGNED WITH YOU IN MIND!

INSPIRATIONAL READING

BOOKS BY JAMES O. DAVIS

www.JamesODavis.com/Store

INTERACTIVE TRAINING

More than 150 interactive training courses by renowned Christian leaders from every major world region!

www.GCLC.tv

ROUNDTABLES

Immerse yourself in the creative wisdom of some of North America's leading communicators with pastors from around the world!

www.PREACH.tv

CONFERENCES

Meet many of the foremost sermonizers, aggressive soul-winners and top missions-minded leaders in the world today.

www.SYNERGIZE.tv

Dr. James O. Davis is founder of Cutting Edge International and the cofounder of Billion Soul Network, comprising more than 500,000 churches. Dr. Davis resides in the greater Orlando area with his wife, Sheri, and daughters, Olivia and Priscilla. They also have two children, Jennifer and James, who reside in heaven.

www.JamesODavis.com

CUTTING EDGE INTERNATIONAL

Cutting Edge International is not about egos and logos, but synergizing the efforts of key Christian leaders for the fulfillment of the Great Commission. From its founding in 1984, Cutting Edge International has been about bringing the "best" in the world to the "rest" in the world.

Our financial base consists of local churches and Christians who are committed to helping us network with every major stream of Christianity for eternal rewards.

PARTNER WITH US!

$20 PER MONTH HELPS US TO NETWORK WITH OTHERS TO PLANT ONE CHURCH!

$20/Month (12 churches/year) · **$100/Month** (60 churches/year)

$250/Month (150 churches/year) · **$500/Month** (300 churches/year)

$1,000/Month (600 churches/year)

"We are witnessing an unparalleled missional shift worldwide. The Global Church is moving from parenting to partnering like never before. I can say with unequivocal confidence that our Lord has raised up this ministry to help network the Body of Christ together for the fulfillment of the Great Commission. Yet, we realize that no single organization can accomplish this alone. Every $20 invested on a monthly basis empowers us to network in the planting of one church. Will you consider partnering with us? I invite you to join with us in the global effort."

James O. Davis
Founder/Cutting Edge International

www.JamesODavis.com

a minute, but eternity is in it. When we rise in the morning, I recommend that we begin first and foremost realizing that this is the day that the Lord has made, and we will rejoice and be glad in it.

Secondly, we have a **present day**. Notice the psalmist did not say this *will be* a day or this *was* the day. He said this *is* the day. This is the day that the Lord has made. It wasn't past tense or future but present tense. There are two days that will take the joy out of today. Do you know what those two days are? Those two days are yesterday and tomorrow. So many people spend their time in yesterday or in tomorrow that they fail to enjoy the moment of today. I love the simplicity of children. They know how to maximize the moment, to enjoy the moment in that day. It is the old-fashioned cliché, take time "to smell the roses" along life's path before you.

Many of us need to unhook ourselves from yesterday. I like what the apostle Paul said in Philippians so many years ago. He said, "I am forgetting those things which are behind me." Paul refused to live in the past. There were many things in Paul's life from which he had to unhook. He had to unhook himself from past guilt. He spoke of himself as the chiefest of all sinners, but he refused to be haunted by the ghost of guilt. He also had to unhook himself from past glory. He was a man who achieved much. Some call him the greatest apostle, but he didn't live in the glory of yesterday. He got up looking forward to today.

Not only did he have to let go of past guilt and past glory, but also past grief. He had suffered a lot, but he refused to sit around, lick his wounds, and talk about how bad and wicked life was. He also had to let go of past grudges. He had been mistreated, stoned, ridiculed, maligned, persecuted, left for dead on two or three occasions, and yet he was willing to put that in the grave of God's forgetfulness. I want to ask you to do the same thing. Don't pull around the load of yesterday. Forget those things which are behind.

There is another day that can rob us of the joy of today, and that is tomorrow. Did you know so many people are simply enduring today trying to get to tomorrow? Many years ago there was a researcher and psychologist, William Martinson, who surveyed three thousand people. He found out that of those three thousand people, 94 percent of them were enduring today to get to tomorrow. They were living their lives waiting for tomorrow. Ladies complained about their children saying, "When they're gone one day, I'll enjoy." It was always a future tense instead of living in today.

Don't pull around the load of yesterday.
Forget those things which are behind.

Let me tell you another way that tomorrow can eat the joy out of today. Not only can we be waiting for tomorrow, but we can also be worrying about tomorrow. Do you know what our Lord said on the Sermon on the Mount? Our Lord said, "Take no thought of tomorrow for tomorrow shall take thought for the things of itself." He said, "Sufficient unto the day is the evil thereof."

What happens when we reach into tomorrow and borrow trouble from it? We begin to worry. That's the interest we pay on borrowed trouble. We reach into tomorrow and we bring tomorrow's trouble into today. But God has not given us strength for tomorrow's problems. God has only given us strength for today's problems, for He said in the book of Deuteronomy, "As your days are, so shall your strength be." God didn't give me strength for tomorrow. If I use today's strengths on tomorrow's problems, then I'll meet tomorrow out of breath because I expended my strength trying to handle today's problems and tomorrow's problems with only today's strength.

Worry doesn't take the sorrow out of tomorrow. Worry takes the strength out of today. I heard about a man who was a constant worrier. Everything went bad for him. The man had a bad job, he wasn't making much money, he drove a rattletrap automobile, his children were failing in school; everything was going downhill for him. One day he straightened up and changed dramatically. He dressed up, smiled, came to work standing tall, and a friend said, "I've never seen such a dramatic change. What changed you? What made the difference? Why don't you worry anymore?" The man said, "Well, I've learned about a remarkable thing. I've learned about a company that has some professional worriers, and what you do is you pay these people and tell one of them about your problems. Then you go off and do your business and they will stay and worry for you. You don't have to worry anymore. You just tell them and pay them." His friend said, "That's marvelous. How much does it cost?" He said, "It costs $1,000 a week." His friend said, "How are you going to pay for that?" He said, "Well, that's their worry."

Let me tell you something, friends. Wouldn't it be wonderful if there was someone who would worry for us, someone who would carry our burdens? Well, I want you to know there is, and His name is Jesus Christ. Jesus said to roll our burdens over onto Him and He would take care of them. Yesterday is a cancelled check. Tomorrow is a promissory note. Today is the only cash we have. We should spend it wisely.

Third, we have a **priceless day**. The Bible says, "This is the day that the Lord hath made," right? It says the Lord hath made it, and therefore it is a priceless day. Have you ever purchased an expensive gift for someone, maybe using much time and energy to do so. However, after you gave the gift, you saw the gift lying around or being mistreated and you thought to yourself, the person doesn't even know how valuable it is or how much effort it took. Well, I think sometimes the Lord looks at how carelessly we use the days He gives to us. The days that God has given to us are priceless. I remind you again that God doesn't have to take life from you. All He has to do is stop giving you another day.

Yesterday is a cancelled check.
Tomorrow is a promissory note.
Today is the only cash we have.
We should spend it wisely.

There is enough time in every day to gracefully do everything God wants us to do, and don't insult the Lord by saying, "I don't have enough time." We have enough time to do the things that God has chosen for us to do. Let me tell you how I begin my day. I begin my day first of all with prayer before the Lord. It is important for me to get "orders from headquarters." It is important for me to know what the Lord has for me for that day. Sometimes I spend longer in prayer than other days, but I want to go out into the day fully focused on what God has planned for me today. Coming on the heels of the prayer are priorities. We cannot do everything and we cannot be everywhere. Sometimes people even have to do things for us or they will not get done. We must learn to set priorities.

One of the greatest challenges in life is not necessarily between the bad and the good, but between the good and the best. Good things become bad things when they keep us from the best things that God has for us. I don't have time to read the good books; I only have time to read the best books. I don't have time to think just the good thoughts; I want to think the best thoughts. I want to maximize every day.

As we prepare for each day, we need to realize that we need power. The apostle Paul would write in the book of

Ephesians that "we are to redeem the time for the days are evil," and in the next verse he would say, "Be filled with the Holy Spirit." That's always been interesting to me. Why would He would connect redeeming time and walking in the Holy Spirit? Well, I believe it's simple. When we're walking in the Holy Spirit, we'll be doing the things that we should be doing and we won't have the time to do things we should not be doing. Therefore, we will redeem the time in an evil age.

How do you handle priceless days? I don't know how many days have transpired before today and I don't know how many days will take place in the future. Yet, there is only one "today." When we go to a world-class museum, we can see rare, priceless artifacts. They are considered priceless due to the quantity and who created them. There is only one Mona Lisa in the Louvre Museum in Paris, France. There is only one statue of David in the Galleria dell'Accademia museum in Florence, Italy. It does not matter how much money a person has, he or she does not have enough to purchase these works of art. They are priceless!

Who is the creator of this day? God. How many days are like today? One. Today is priceless due to who created it and because there is one of them. We are to handle priceless days with reverence, humility, and prayer. Sometimes I wonder how God feels when we waste priceless days on valueless pursuits.

Fourth, we have a **passing day**. This is the day that the Lord has made. This day is quickly passing by, and it will be buried in the tomb of time forever. There are several things you cannot do with time. You can't borrow, take, or loan time. You can't give time or put it in a bottle or a bank. You can't take time out of the game of life. There are only two things that you can do with time, and that is you can either use time or lose time. I can't give you my time and you can't give me your time. I can't take or borrow time. All I can do with time is either use it or lose it.

> When as I child I laughed and wept, time crept.
> When as a youth I dreamed and talked, time walked.
> When I became a full-grown man, time ran.
> When older still I daily grew, time flew.
> Soon I shall find myself traveling on, time gone....
>
> —Henry Twells[5]

Are you going to do something significant for God? Then I'd recommend you get started. Are you going to become a prayer warrior? You'd better start praying. Are you going to memorize those Bible verses? You'd better start learning them. Are you going to become a soul winner and win people to Jesus? There's no better time than today. Are you going to grow up and mature and believe God for awesome things? Well, you better start growing and maturing today. You see, there's no better time than this very moment.

Some time ago a lady was asking a friend of hers whether or not she should go to college. Her friend responded, "Why should you not go?" The lady replied, "It will take four years to go to college, and I'll be forty years old when I get out." Her friend said, "Well, how old will you be if you don't go to college?" The issue is not whether or not you're going to go to college. The issue is if that's what the Lord has for you to do, you ought to get started with it today.

Last, we have **providential** day. The Bible says, "This is the day that the Lord has made." Today has God's providence wrapped around it. God overrules today. Nothing is going to come to me that doesn't first come through Jesus Christ. I want you to know that the sovereign God is in charge of the affairs of this world, and not a blade of grass moves without

[5] "Henry Twells Quote," iz quotes, http://izquotes.com/quote/352804.

His permission. Do you know what the secret of joy is? Listen to what the psalmist said, "This is the day that the Lord has made. I will rejoice and be glad in it." Do you know what the secret of joy is? It is to see the providence of God in everything and thank Him for it.

The Word of God says we are to give thanks, for this is God's will concerning us (1 Thessalonians 5:18). Philippians 4:6-7 says, "Be careful of nothing; but in everything by prayer and supplication with thanksgiving let your requests be made known to God. And the peace of God, which passes all understanding, will keep your hearts and minds through Jesus Christ." Ephesians 5:20 says, "Give thanks always for all things...."

Good things become bad things when they keep us from the best things that God has for us.

The secret of joy in today is to see God's fingertips in the day and understand that God's providence is in the midst of your day. Providence means to see ahead of time. Before the sun rose on the beauty of this day, God saw it. God doesn't need to put His signature in the bottom of the day because He's the owner. He doesn't have to put His signature on the hillside of the day because He is the owner.

Did you know you can choose to be happy and you can choose to be unhappy? There are some people who just enjoy being miserable. I think it would be wonderful if there was somewhere we could lock them all up and let them worry themselves to death. They just seem like they want to be unhappy. Do you know that you can resolutely say, "This is the day that the Lord has made and I will rejoice and be glad in it"? In our hearts we thank Him for the sun, but do we thank Him for the rain? We thank Him for joy, but do we thank Him for pain? We thank Him for gains, but do we thank Him for losses? We thank Him for blessings, but do we thank Him for the crosses? In everything give thanks, for this is the will of God in Christ Jesus concerning you.

This is the day that the Lord has made and we will rejoice and be glad in it. Let me tell you what I've been trying to say. Do you want to make this the greatest day of your life? Do you want to maximize every day? Live in the eternal now. Today is the only day you have. Stop saying, "If I had time." You have the time. Unhook yourself from yesterday, quit waiting for tomorrow, and live today for the glory of God. For if you would let every God-given day become a God-governed day, it will become a God-gladdened day, and you'll be able to say, "This is the day that the Lord has made, and I will rejoice and be glad in it."

Unhook yourself from yesterday, quit waiting for tomorrow, and live today for the glory of God.

In August of 2007, I was fortunate to make a trip to Auckland, New Zealand, to see Sir Edmund Hillary. Sir Edmund Hillary is the one who climbed Mt. Everest in 1953 before anyone else. While I was with Sir Edmund Hillary and his lovely wife, Lady June, we had a wonderful conversation. I found that he was a very godly, wise gentleman. During our time together, we discussed the issues of time and how quickly it was passing by.

I made the comment about how difficult procrastination is for many people to overcome. At that time Sir Edmund Hillary was eighty-eight years old, and within a few months he would pass away. This was the last interview he would grant anyone outside of his family. I considered myself most fortunate to spend almost two-and-a-half hours with him in his home.

I looked into his eyes and I said to him, "You talked about time and you talked about the importance in doing whatever it is we're going to do right now. Why is it so important that we do it right now?" He paused for a moment, and then he continued in his conversation. He said, "I'm eighty-eight years old now, and there are six things that I will not be able to accomplish." I looked at him and I said, "Would you please mind telling me what one of those things would be?" And he responded, "In 1956 I was the first one to ever cross Antarctica." He said, "James, some say crossing Antarctica was harder than crossing Mt. Everest." Of course, I had no way of knowing which was the hardest because I've never climbed Mt. Everest and I've never crossed Antarctica.

He said, "When I was crossing the bottom of the earth, I had scaled a mountain range. I stood on it and I looked across a glacier filled with ice and animal life and I said to myself, *Hike down this mountain, crawl across this ice, scale the other mountain range, and see the view from the other side.* I said to myself, *I'm a fairly young man. I'll come back and do that another day.* He said, "Well, that young man has become an old man, and I will never go back to Antarctica. I will never scale that mountain range. I will never cross that ice filled with animal life and scale the other mountain and see the view from the other side."

He said there are two seasons in every person's life. There is a season when time and energy work for you; and there is a season when time and energy work against you. But one does not know what season he or she is in until he or she tries to accomplish a project that's bigger than themselves. It will be at that moment you will come to understand whether or not you are in the season when time and energy work for you, or in the season that time and energy work against you.

Therefore, whatever it is you're going to do, do it now. Choose your biggest projects now. Leverage time and energy now to achieve what is in your heart.

I would like to ask you, what is it that God has put in your heart? What is that God-given vision and dream that the Lord has placed within you? You better get started now. Leverage time and energy for your favor and for your labor, because one day that time and energy will work against you. A little later, we were in Sir Edmund's small kitchen and he was signing some books for me. I had asked him to sign three books, and I believe I have the last three books he ever signed in my library.

Conquer life's challenges and realize how precious this day is. Then go out and do something great for our Lord and Savior.

I couldn't happen but notice his hands shaking as he was holding the book and signing my name, and I thought to myself that time and energy were working against him to the point that it was hard to hold a book; it was hard to sign his name. There was a time when those same hands would scale Mt. Everest six miles high or cross Antarctica, but now time and energy were working against him.

I challenge you to make every day a God-given day so that it might be a God-gladdened day. Conquer life's challenges and realize how precious this day is. Then go out and do something great for our Lord and Savior.

Invitation: You Can Do It!

Since the initial launch of the Billion Soul Network in 2002, four overarching phases have been taking place to synergize pastors and leaders together toward the doubling of the size of the global church in our generation.

First, the *discovery phase* occurred with the intentionality of finding out who Christ is raising up around the world in order to tie relational knots for enormous harvest. Billion Soul Summits were conducted in every world region, with more than ten thousand global leaders being interviewed face-to-face to find out what the Lord is up to in the twenty-first century. Our Lord gave me the strength to attend every summit!

On the heels of the discovery phase came the *development phase,* with the creating of an international curriculum for pastors/leaders in every nation. Each of the teachers contributed their best training to the global church. John Corts, former president of the Billy Graham Evangelistic Association for twenty-five years, and Dr. Elmer Towns, Cofounder of Liberty University, provided the leadership necessary to create and craft this powerful online training curriculum.

Once the discovery and development phases were sizable and sustainable, the *distribution phase* was launched through the *Global Church Learning Center* (www.GCLC.tv). Included in the GCLC are the Global Church Classroom (consisting of 150 powerful and practical courses) and the Global Church

Library (with hundreds of additional resources). The international response has been enormous!

With all of these previous phases dynamically functioning, in 2012 BSN moved into the *deployment phase*. The deployment phase involved the launching of *Global HUBS of Christianity*. The overall function of a HUB is to:

- Synergize the Best Relationships
- Systematize the Best Resources
- Strategize for the Unreached People Groups

The global church is moving from production to reproduction. The greatest missional shift of our generation is summed up in this statement: "The mission field has become a mission force!"

Do you believe everything you read in the newspaper? I hope the answer is, "No." Do you believe everything you read in the Bible? I hope the answer is, "Yes!" Do you spend more time reading things you don't believe compared to the things you do believe?

How much of the world do you believe Jesus died for? I hope you believe He died for the whole world. Do you have a God-sized vision that embraces the entirety of the world, with a plan to fulfill it in your lifetime? When we take ownership of a God-sized vision, we will quickly realize that we cannot fulfill it by ourselves.

The Billion Soul Story is not so much about a goal to be achieved as it is a role to be believed. This global network was launched by two Christian men, who came from two totally different backgrounds and two different generations. The stated goal of the Billion Soul Network is to help plant five million new churches for a Billion Soul harvest. Yet the role this network plays is to help bring countless numbers of Christians together to build relationships, share resources, and give recommendations for greater success in the whole body of Christ.

Do you know your role in the body of Christ? Have you prayed about it? When we take the Great Commission literally and seriously, we will then have to move from goal-setting to role-setting in our lives. One goal, countless roles!

I must admit in the early years of launching this enormous pastors' network, how we would fully accomplish this in our lifetime was unclear. There were many financial, relational, national, and international challenges before us. My friend and cofounder was struggling for every breath and would graduate to eternity within two and a half years after the beginning of this global network.

Sooner or later, every visionary leader will face his midnight hour of the soul. If no one has ever fought against you, then probably your vision is not worth fighting for.

There were many nay-sayers on one side and many yea-sayers on the other side. It was a constant tug-of-war. I watched people come with their own hidden agendas, disguised in different fashions. Yet, one by one they came, and one by one they left. I remember like it was yesterday, a particular person applauded the effort in front of others in a meeting to only tell me privately by phone that he was against this global vision. On another occasion, I witnessed a well-known person raising money in our green room for his organization at our Billion Soul event! I watched pastors and leaders make financial pledge commitments in front of others as to not be outdone by someone else. Then, when they left for home, they never did send one dollar of their commitment to us.

I remember in December 2006, lying on the floor in an Orlando condo we were leasing with my face in the carpet, broken, lonely, and fearful, asking the Lord what He wanted me to do with the vision He had placed into my mind and heart. It was in the middle of the darkness of that awful night that the Lord gave me a plan of execution. When I gained enough strength to rise to my feet, I decided by faith that I would walk this vision out day by day until it came to pass in my generation. It is in moments like this that we come face-to-face as to whether or not what we are doing is a "day dream" or a "divine vision." From December 2006, until the end of December 2008, we waged spiritual warfare while walking this God-given vision out on a daily basis. My hair turned gray in a few short months. Sooner or later, every visionary leader will face his midnight hour of the soul. If no one has ever fought against you, then probably your vision is not worth fighting for.

When you come to realize what your role in God's goal is, then you become focused on that goal, and many of the things that used to matter to you don't matter anymore. Shortly thereafter, I "faith-tuned" a list of ten steps to global networking success. After I wrote them down, I continued to pray over them and rearranged several of them. Once I knew exactly the sequence of the steps to take, I got up every day knowing exactly what to do. It did not matter what others did and did not do or what others said or did not say, I stayed on the steps before me. In those early days, I did not know exactly how long each step would take, but knew with the Lord's insight and the Holy Spirit's strength, each step would be accomplished, and momentum would be ours for years to come. I give the Lord praise when I say that all ten steps on the path to global networking success were completed in 2012. I am not implying that we no longer face challenges, for we continue to do so as we navigate our way through the diverse international landscape before us.

We need to remember the unbreakable promises of God. In the book of Genesis, when Joseph was a young man, the

Lord revealed a futuristic vision to him. Even though he did not fully understand all of the future ramifications, he began walking out his life with the end in mind. When God gives you a vision, be careful with whom you initially share that vision. Joseph shared with his brothers, and they were the ones who turned on him and threw him into a pit to be sold into slavery. While we are looking for our enemies, from time to time we need to assess those who are closest to us. The closest ones to us will determine the level of success.

Even though Joseph was second in command, he was in that leadership position to build the transition for God's people into the future.

Even though Joseph was not originally included in the promise that God made to Abraham (Gen. 15:12-16), he would live his life according to the promise made to Abraham. God told Abraham that he would have a Son (Isaac) and that his son would become a great nation. Over a period of time, this nation would move to Egypt and become slaves there. However, after 400 years, God would bring them out (the Exodus) and lead them into the Promised Land.

Joseph lived his life on a higher level. Joseph was sold into slavery and eventually ended up working in Potiphar's house. There came a time when Potiphar's wife tempted Joseph, but he ran from that temptation. He left his coat but took his character with him! At any rate, Joseph was falsely accused and thrown into prison. While he was in prison, he did not play the blame game, but simply kept the vision alive in his heart and eventually gained favor in prison. Then one day the big opportunity happened!

Joseph was able to interpret dreams in prison and subsequently interpreted the dream of Pharaoh. Pharaoh recognized that the Spirit of God was upon Joseph's life. This is the first reference in the Bible of the Spirit of God resting upon a person's life. All along the way, from the pit to the prison to the palace, Joseph continued to fulfill his role in God's goal for his generation. He knew what God was up to, and he was connecting the present with the future for the saving of an entire generation. Joseph knew what his role was and understood what God's goal was for His people. Our roles are usually deeper than our professions. Even though Joseph was second in command, he was in that leadership position to build the transition for God's people into the future.

We need to rely on the unshakable power of God. Companies open and they close. Denominations start and they stop. Empires are raised up and they come down. Yet, the Kingdom of God continues to grow each year. There are concerns around us and changes coming toward us. Joseph's concern was that he about to die (Gen. 5:22-26). With his passing, a seismic change was coming to the Israelites. They were moving from favor to labor.

Throughout our lives, we are to depend upon the resources of the Lord. When we are called and commissioned to achieve something bigger than ourselves or to set a rippling effect into the next generation, our faith will be stretched beyond our comprehension.

Joseph knew that the Exodus was just beyond his lifetime. Thus, when he was dying, he pulled his family together and reminded them of what the Lord was going to take them through some day. Joseph was so certain that he made them promise him they would take him with them!

We need to rest in the unmistakable peace of God. When the Exodus finally did come under the leadership of Moses, Joseph was taken with them and carried in a box for more than fifty years until he made it to Canaan! Moses commanded that Joseph be brought out of Egypt (Ex. 13:17-19). He as carried throughout the entire wilderness wanderings for forty years and then he was brought into the Promised Land. After the Canaan wars were over, Joseph was buried in Shechem (Josh. 24:32-33).

Why did Joseph make his family promise to take him with them? He wanted to be a part of what God was doing, whether he was dead or alive! Can you say this? Are you willing to fulfill your role in God's goal, regardless of whether it is easy or hard, pleasurable or painful? Joseph had faith beyond the grave and could see his people inheriting the Promised Land. He set events in motion that would move an entire nation into their divine destiny.

Become larger! Think bigger! Pray deeper! Listen harder! Love longer! See further! Live wider! Believe higher! This is your time!

Could it be that the Lord is giving you an invitation to believe Him for the greatest vision of your life? Are you willing to move from goal-setting to role-setting? Regardless of the ministry vocation or business profession, you have a role in God's goal. If you are in ministry, then the challenge is for you to take ownership of the Great Commission and begin to realign your time and energy toward devoting a certain amount that truly helps those to hear the Gospel who have never heard before. If you are in business, then you need to be able to get on your knees with integrity, asking God to prosper your business because you have chosen to contribute value toward those who have never heard the Gospel for the first time. Each of us has a role in the goal!

I extend this invitation to you. Become larger! Think bigger! Pray deeper! Listen harder! Love longer! See further! Live wider! Believe higher! This is your time! In the future those who are networking will eventually be not working! I look forward to seeing you on the roof of the world, where we together place the cross of Christ high enough for all the world to see, understand, and respond to it.

Afterword

You will have untold billions of thoughts during your lifetime with only a small percentage of them becoming ideas. Ideas planted in people's minds have reaping consequences. These consequences comprise the evil and good outcomes in our lives, communities, nation, and world. We can choose our choices but not our consequences!

So often today our culture seems to be wrestling with "What is truth?" rather than "Who is truth?" *The Billion Soul Story: Finding Your Role In God's Goal* has not been written to explain the "what" but to bring focus on the "who." I do not pretend to think or speak for you, but it seems we spend a lot of time cursing the darkness instead of lighting a candle. The simple reason for more darkness in Western civilization is because there is less light today. If Christians were simply to become who they are supposed to be, there would be less darkness in the future.

Can you imagine what would happen if all of the Christians in the West won and discipled just one person in the next twelve months? The radical change from more darkness to more light would be evident in our education, vocation, and nation. It is the power of mature, Christ-centered ideas that can help save the world from self-destruction.

Our heavenly Father, the King of the universe, had a God-sized thought before time began or creation emerged out of nothing. Contained in this thought was the future birth of His Son, Jesus, the God-man, who would be the bridge between mankind and God. Yet this God-idea was not finished yet.

Words are the outward thoughts of our lives. Jesus was the outward expression of the inward thoughts of His Father. No wonder John stated in his gospel that the "Word became flesh" (1:14). Jesus epitomizes the idea of redemption for the whole world.

So much has changed throughout the earth during this generation, but basic human motivations remain the same. On the one hand, I am a member of the last generation who will be able to recall typewriters before computers, and payphones before cell phones—just to name a few. On the other hand, my wife Debbie and I have raised amazing children, who are giving us grandchildren who have the possibility of seeing the twenty-second century!

The Billion Soul Story has shown you that Christianity is not about to go out of business in our world today. The global Church is growing faster now than any previous generation. I have often heard Dr. James O. Davis, cofounder of the Billion Soul Network, speak with amazing clarity as to who our Lord is raising up around the world. In this powerful book you have read and learned terms and phrases that include the "Global Hubs of Christianity," "the rise of the Global Church," "the new face of Christianity," "moving from the best to the rest," "the circumference of Christianity," "find your role in God's goal" and so much more.

It has been a joy of mine to minister at the biennial Synergize Pastors & Leaders Conferences and to partner with the Billion Soul Network, both in the United States and abroad. As Dr. Davis and I synergize our efforts together in the years ahead, we will be articulating a clarion call of moving the Church to synergistically network together toward the fulfillment of the Great Commission.

We believe God's Word instructs us that the best is yet to come for the Body of Christ. Instead of standing on the curb of time, watching the parade of God's promises march by us, let's decide to get out front and lead the Church, like never before, into the unlimited number of victories in this generation!

Dr. Glenn Burris
President
Foursquare International
Los Angeles, CA
October 2015

About the Author

Dr. James O. Davis founded Cutting Edge International and cofounded the Billion Soul Network, a growing coalition of more than two thousand Christian ministries and denominations. This coalition is synergizing its efforts to build a premier community of pastors worldwide to help plant five million new churches for a billion soul harvest. The Billion Soul Network, with more than 500,000 churches, has become the largest pastors' network in the world.

Christian leaders recognize Dr. Davis as the leading networker in the Christian world. More than fifty thousand pastors and leaders have attended his biannual pastors' conference, preaching roundtables, and leadership summits across the United States and in all major world regions. He has been named in *Top Ten Christian Influencers in the World* and as "Leader of the Year."

Dr. Davis served twelve years leading 1,500 evangelists and training thousands of students for full-time evangelism as the National Evangelists Representative at the Assemblies of God world headquarters. Ministering more than forty-five weeks per year for more than thirty years to an average yearly audience of 150,000 people, he has now traveled over eight million miles to minister face-to-face to more than eight million people in more than 115 nations.

Dr. Davis earned a Doctorate in Ministry in Preaching at Trinity Evangelical Divinity School and two master's degrees from the Assemblies of God Theological Seminary. In addition to writing numerous books, he has published articles and been quoted in *Charisma, Ministry Today, The Challenge Weekly, The New York Times Magazine,* and elsewhere. He resides in the Orlando area with his wife, Sheri, and daughters, Olivia and Priscilla. They have two children, Jennifer and James, who reside in heaven. For more information on Dr. Davis, Cutting Edge International, and Billion Soul Network, visit:

www.jamesodavis.com
and
www.billion.tv

More Dynamic Books by Dr. James O. Davis

We Are the Church: The Untold Story of God's Global Awakening
(with Dr. Leonard Sweet)

How to Make Your Net Work:
Tying Relational Knots for Global Impact

Scaling Your Everest: Lessons from Sir Edmund Hillary

Gutenberg to Google:
The Twenty Indispensable Laws of Communication

What to Do When the Lights Go Out

Signposts on the Road to Armageddon

It's a Miraculous Life!

12 Big Ideas

Living Like Jesus

The Pastor's Best Friend: The New Testament Evangelist

The Preacher's Summit

Beyond All Limits: The Synergistic Church for a Planet in Crisis
(with Dr. Bill Bright)

Personal Note Page
Discovering My Role in God's Goal

Personal Note Page

Discovering My Role in God's Goal

Personal Note Page

Discovering My Role in God's Goal

Personal Note Page
Discovering My Role in God's Goal

Personal Note Page

Discovering My Role in God's Goal

Personal Note Page

Discovering My Role in God's Goal

Personal Note Page

Discovering My Role in God's Goal